1

Buttermilk Book Publishing

Myrtle Beach, South Carolina

This book is the author's journey into a relationship with God. All incidences and references are as they occurred and as documented within a journal kept by the author. Some references are indicated from media posts as they related to his journey.

Typecast in Times New Roman

ISBN 978-1-7365555-1-4

Dedication

God Our Savior

My wife, Judy for her prayers, patience, for believing in me and for proofing book.

Reverend Dr. William 'Buddy' Phillips for his wisdom and guidance.

Sammy Cannon, Cuz, My Brother for his ultimate sacrifice and for starting the ball rolling.

Judy Cannon, for volunteering to proof this book and forever loving Sammy.

Pushed into The Pull
Thank You Cuz

God reminds us that:
He will make a way for us.
He is fighting our battles.
Prayer is the best medicine.
Trust in His timing.

Preface

Samuel Atticus Cannon (Sammy) was born April 8, 1950. He had always been my cousin, who later became my friend, my Cuz and eventually My Brother. Being an only child, myself, having Sammy as a brother was huge in my life. We shared much in too short a time, at age sixty-seven his life on earth was brought to an untimely ending by an incurable disease, chronic myelomonocyte leukemia. He gained his glorious angel wings February 17, 2018. I had begun writing about Cuz as my way to cope and heal from losing someone I so loved, but what a journey it has been. I documented this in a book I later published titled *Cuz My Brother, Life is Good, God is Good*. His family and friends contributed as well with wonderful memories. Writing that tribute book took me places that I was not prepared to go. Even in death life can offer purpose. Sammy's death introduced me to something I had never experienced. Dealing with this tragic loss I found life, a relationship with God that I had never had. Imagine, a man in his sixties, who had never understood his purpose in this world and one who believed in God but had never experienced a life with God. That book was published June 8, 2018. Now begins a new chapter, different book, one with a powerful message and a T. Allen Winn awakening. It began innocently enough as a journal after publishing the book, a vessel for capturing my feelings in a spiritual journey. Oh, how it became much more, so much so that I felt compelled to share it. My journey is but my journey, one many have experienced, and it probably is not unique to anyone but me. God always has a plan for us. Maybe, just maybe, this one is from His playbook. It is my story to tell so here goes, blaming it on Cuz, his death guiding me toward something unexpectedly wonderful. It started as my journal, my reflections, my struggle to understand.

I will lift up mine eyes unto the hills,
From whence cometh my help.
My help cometh from the Lord,
Which made heaven and earth.
Psalm 121:1-2

Forward

Judy Cannon, Cuz's bride, saw a preview of this book that I posted on Facebook under The Beach Author Network Group. I had failed to give her a heads up that I had written and was publishing this book. She responded online to the posting.

Oh my, Tommy, I had no idea that you were writing this. Sammy is truly looking down and saying, "pour me one more beer in the funnel, Cuz!" He was truly a man of God and he loved you unconditionally. I still shiver when I think of the two of you disagreeing on something, thinking you would hate each other, but ending up as if the conversation never happened.

How I miss him EVERY SINGLE DAY. But just to know he was instrumental in saving one soul (yours) makes my loss a definite plus. Thank you for being such an instrumental part of Sammy's life.

Moments after this post, Judy also sent me a text.

I am sitting in my bed bawling my eyes out. I am missing my Sammy so much. When I saw your new book, I knew beyond a shadow of a doubt that his death resulted into a miracle – your salvation. We are going to have one big rejoicing party someday. So, I must have four books, one for me, and one for each of Sammy's girls. Man, I miss him. There is just no simple solution to grief.

I am so thankful, Tommy. I have so many memories especially, of the two of you. I am so happy he inspired this book. If you need someone to proof it, I will (between the tears.)

And just like that, Judy Cannon did indeed proof this book.

Steps in the Journey

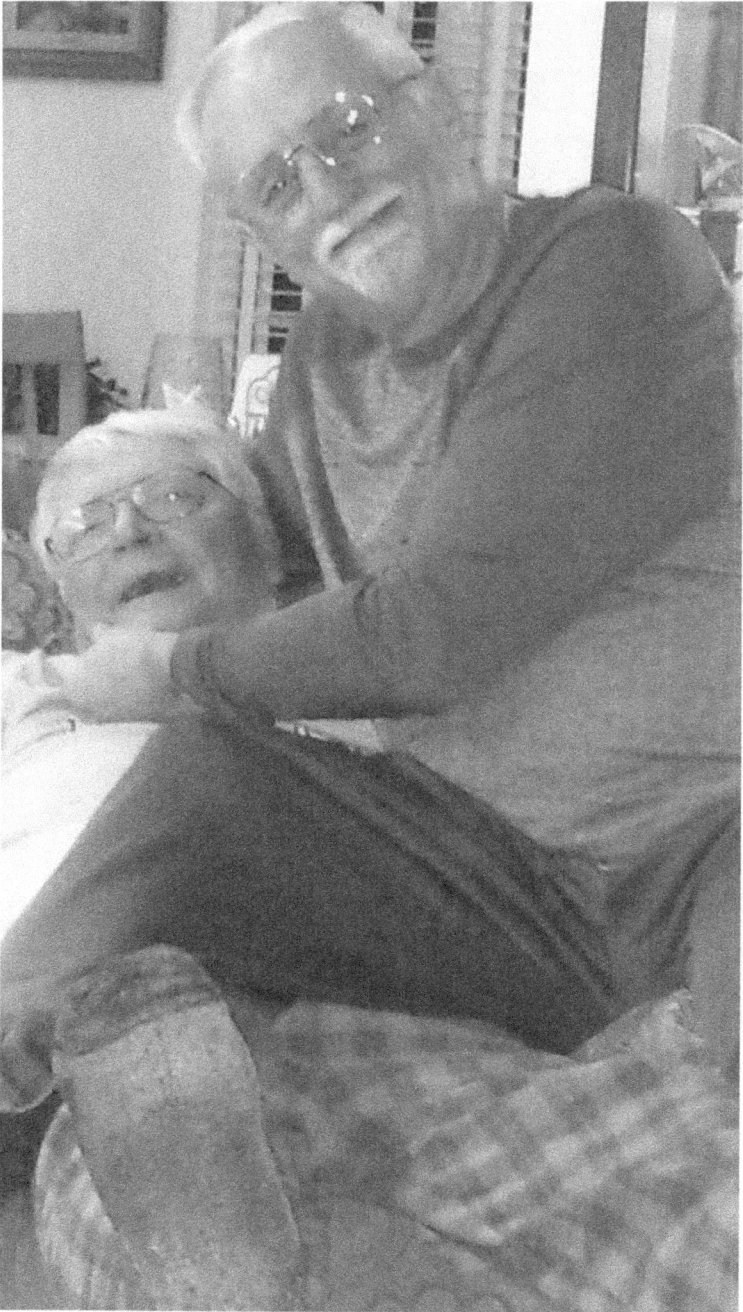

From the archives, Cuz and Me

Lessons Learned If You Open Your Heart and Listen

My plan had been to end the Sammy Cannon tribute with his Judy's memories in that first book. My plan was not His plan apparently. And in His I am not talking about Sammy Cannon, Cuz, My Brother this time. Although, I do believe Cuz played an intricate part in it. I have been impacted beyond measure by Sammy's passing. In our hearts we knew it was inevitable but the inevitable just was not supposed to have happened this quickly. I have grieved too, but I have shared that grief throughout that tribute book of the man I loved as a brother. We all have. But for me it has been different. You might ask how mine can be different or unique from everyone else's. I will try to explain. Sammy's death put something in motion, a slow-moving train, something I am still coping with and trying to understand. I have struggled with Sammy's death for months now. But what I have been trying to do is learn from what happened to him and how it has impacted me. I have not sorted it out yet but here is what I have learned, especially after reading Judy Cannon's journey of grieving. Life is precious. Time is precious. We never know if we have another second or another minute or another day.

Sunday, April 29, 2018, we headed to church, all normal from that perspective. We took the back exit from our neighborhood in Myrtle Beach to Business Highway 17. At the stop sign we waited for an opening to cross 17 and head north to First Methodist Church ten minutes away. We made it to the cross over and waited as two convertible sports cars in both lanes passed and then we pulled out behind them. Pirate Land Campground is the next cross over less than a hundred yards away. A truck pulling a twenty-eight-foot trailer decided to cross the north bound lanes blocking both as it came to a complete stop. The sports cars traveling maybe forty-five or fifty miles an hour have seemingly no place to go, a certain double T-bone unavoidable. One makes a miraculous maneuver veering into the entrance to the campground that the truck just exited, while the second car somehow veers through the same crossover that the truck pulling the camper is occupying and completes a U-turn in front of southbound traffic. I am breaking behind them awestruck how the big one didn't happen and thankful I wasn't closer and had to make that last second decision in our SUV.

What happened on the way to church this morning furthered the falling of the dominoes. Sammy's passing, Judy's journals setting the first in the sequence of life changes and revelations. It just emphasized how quickly tragedy can strike. That could have been us when that trailer pulled across the road. Only seconds separated us from those cars ahead. Miracle, maybe. And then we attended the church service. Pastor Buddy Phillip's sermon kept this slow-moving train in motion. He shared a personal story of being an eighteen-year-old paramedic arriving on the scene of an accident, a truck T-boning a car and the car flipping on its top. They could not locate the driver of the car, thinking maybe he or she ran off. Buddy then discovered that the driver was penned underneath the top of the car. It took quite some time to safely lift the car without crushing the person underneath. Once they did, tragedy struck. The car with the pressure of its weight had been preventing the driver from hemorrhaging. The driver bled to death once rescued.

Buddy noticed a tiny hand protruding from the mangled and crushed backseat door. They freed the child. Holding the child in his arms, he delivered him to the ER and then waited to hear the outcome. He smoked a pipe and waited for nearly an hour until the doctor stepped out and said the child did not make it. Buddy said he was overwhelmed by the outcome and threw up, then walked outside and looked skyward and asked, "Where the hell were You?" He was angry with God for not saving the child after already witnessing the father's death. His sermon's message ends four years later when he receives his answer from God in a church service, that God tells him He is there to protect his family.

So, you again might ask why I am sharing this story and what it has to do with Sammy, My Brother. Connecting the dots, Sammy's death, Judy's journal, the near miss and now Buddy's message touched me as much as anything has ever touched me before. I have never been good at talking about this sort of stuff, the religious part of it. I struggle with this subject, always have. I believe in God. That is not an issue. I have just never had a relationship with God, for reasons too long to cover here, because this is not "all about me" but it has changed me. I do feel for Judy and what she is going through.

16

She would give anything to have what we have in our marriage, each other, another chance. My point, I am getting to it.

Today at church was the nearest connection I guess I have experienced since we have been attending First Church or in my life if truth be known. I don't fully understand it yet, but it registered with me. Chain of events, Sammy's death, listening to his Judy's struggles and then reading her grieving journal have been tearing me apart. I have been experiencing something I cannot explain. It did hit me like a ton of bricks what Buddy experienced with that accident and how he turned to ask God, where were You. It was a revelation for me. Maybe a dent in my armor but it struck me as a beginning. Life is precious, and we should cherish it, right?

Religion! Boy how I have fought it tooth and claw all my life. The more it has been forced my way the more I have fought against it. Resisting has been my defense mechanism. Seems I do that a lot. People often say I seem emotionless. I joke, saying my feelings are inside, often saying I smile or laugh on the inside as well. I know I don't show it as much as I should, keeping it inside, but I do have an emotional heart. This morning I felt something. This is new to me, this connection, or feelings or whatever it might be. Maybe Sammy's death and him then visiting me three times in dreams have been signs of some sort. The last visit was a simple one. I told him I did not want to go, and Sammy said, "Then don't." Maybe God is working through him to save me. There was a time I could not have typed or even said that last sentence. Maybe there is hope for me after all. Possibly Sammy Cannon's death had more purpose than even I can begin to understand.

Writing that tribute book had been the toughest and best book I have ever worked on. Life is Good, God is Good came to me as a catchy Sammy Cannon phrase to use as a subtitle. I am wondering now if there was more to it than just that, the God is Good part especially. Again, I amaze myself because these thoughts do not come easy for me or at least they used to not. People must arrive at their own speed and own time. I have pushed it away and have resisted for so long that even I never thought it was possible. Today might just be a new beginning for me. I know it has consumed me and today I have struggled to understand it. It is so out of the norm for me. The mere fact I mentioned Buddy and his story, his message and being the best sermon that I have ever heard during our 'after church' breakfast with Gene and Rhonda Singleton was a HUGE step for me. I usually sit on the sidelines of religious conversations. I have always figured it was not my place to engage in matters that I did not understand or whole heartily support.

So, what now? I do not know. I am in virgin territory when it comes to this. I don't know exactly how to wrap my head around it. Sammy said it best. Life is Good, God is Good. No. I am not Sammy, nowhere even close and would never want to be Sammy. He is who he was, and I am who I am. So how do I move forward? I don't have those answers either. I wish I did. Others have experienced it. But this is new to me. Am I going to be this perfectly transformed human being now? I have no idea where I go from here. I just know it has struck something in me that I have never experienced. It's almost scary in a way. Not in a bad way but in a much different way for me.

Crazy thoughts from me for sure but Jesus gave His life for us. I am now wondering if the real reason Sammy and I became so close is so that he would be the one that led me to on thus journey to a relationship with God. It sends chills through me for me to even put it this way. What is the saying, God works in mysterious ways? I don't know about all that but what I do know is I've never typed quicker or more deliberately before, never ever in any of my fiction novels. My brain, my heart or whatever you want to call it is connected directly to my fingers and the keyboard. It's like I don't know how to stop, like I'm the only one who has had this happen to them before. Sinners repent and find the righteous path regularly, don't they? I do not have the market cornered on this but for the first time I am engaged. Not of my own choosing but chosen just the same.

I used my smart phone and snapped a photograph while we were in Cracker Barrel this morning of one of those blocks with an inscription on it. It just struck me as important. It read, 'Where there is Life there is Love.' Now I think I understand why. It connects to this message, Sammy, Judy's grieving, the almost wreck and then Buddy, puzzle pieces somehow falling into place. And I have never been one fond of puzzles or good at working them. But here they are, connected and somehow making sense, a message to me, for me. Sammy's tribute has been much more all along. I thought it was the right thing to do and it served as therapy for me or, so I had convinced myself. I was wrong. There was a much bigger picture, one I had not noticed until now. Hit me between the eyes with a two by four, Lord. Thank you very much.

It is going to be better than all right. It has been taken off my shoulders. God is Good, and Our Lives will be Good too. It is funny how I am sitting here smiling, not crying, not fretting, not wondering what I can do next, better do, should do, could have done. It is nice not having to worry about it. How does that song go, *Love Lifted Me*. It is going to really be all right. Everything is going to be okay. I have put my trust in Him who will make sure of that. He certainly has His hands full guiding me along but then it isn't His first rodeo, but it is certainly mine. I have turned the reins over to Him and I am going where the ride takes me. I plan to schedule a meeting with Pastor Buddy Phillips to see what he thinks I should do with this new-found freedom. My Judy suggested me doing this. In the past I would have ignored and avoided such a suggestion, that I talk to a preacher. Oddly, I am open to it for a change. Who knows, maybe I can even learn to smile more on the outside once I maneuver through this obstacle course. Like death, I guess what I am experiencing marches to its own timetable. You cannot force it or pray that God fixes it. It eventually fixes itself with His help when He sees the best place to fit it in. Listen to me. Like I have a clue about stuff like this.

Our journey began as cousins, friends and then brothers. The spiritual journey begins now. I love you My Brother. Life is Indeed Good, God is Better. See you on the other side. Save me a spot in your heavenly golf foursome, Cuz.

'God never takes away something from your life without replacing it with something better.' Billy Graham

Every Start has a Humble Beginning

Abbeville, South Carolina, small town, rich in history, but me, nobody special, just an only child born in 1953 to parents making a living in a mill town. Textile industry flourished in that long ago time. Milliken and Self were prominent names in the textile world, especially in Abbeville and Greenwood counties. Abbeville also had ties to the birth of the confederacy, but this is not a history lesson. It is my journey, wild and reckless at times but one with a purpose possibly. Well, the purpose is in the eye of the beholder and no more significant than that. I am the beholder, mostly without purpose through much of my life, but I am getting ahead of myself.

Thomas Allen Winn named so by my parents to ensure that I would never be pegged as Junior. My dad was Thomas Jefferson Winn. Changing that middle name was supposed to keep folks from calling me Junior. I was just Tommy, through much of my life; Tommy the only child so it ended up being. Life was simple, safe with no political ramifications. Tommy would be quite the little rebel through many of his years granted in the kingdom God created. Unfortunately, I did not think in Godly terms or dwell on His creation. That is a tough row to hoe when the world rotates around your little garden spot in a universe belonging to one who lived a life of fun and recklessness. I pushed it to the limit more times than I can count, a cat with 9 lives and then some. A daredevil knows no boundaries. Testing fate seemed to come way too natural and easy for me. No, I am not bragging; just thinking back now just how miraculous it is for me to still be standing and accounted for.

Was there a greater plan in store for me? Is that why I am still here? How many have asked that question? There is nothing special about me or any abilities I might possess. I am certainly not the disciple type and would never ever profess that destiny holds something uniquely worldly for me. As stated, I am thankful to still be around and in reasonably good shape for an old man. Getting here had its challenges. Mama and Daddy could have testified to that fact if they were still here. No denying it, I added a few grey hairs and worry wrinkles to them with my wild and wooly ways. I can't say I intentionally set out to be on what some might depict as a self-destructive path, but I didn't have the best personal intentions in mind with some of my antics and their outcomes. I sound like I think I was some sort of hoodlum, a badass as some might say. On the contrary, I was far from it. I just did not do anything halfway. It was always choke open and full throttle, no matter what the pointless cause might have been. Like many, I almost felt I was running away from something or at the least, trying to outrun something. What that something was, beats me?

Mama often recapped stories about the tiny tot Tommy that had these daredevil tendencies. She said I was maybe two or three years old when I climbed behind the wheel of the family vehicle while it was idling. I hunkered down, sliding underneath the steering wheel and pressed the gas pedal to the floor, revving the engine wide open. By the grace of God, even back then, I somehow did not manage to shift the car out of neutral. Her words, I would have slammed into the rear of the garage. Just wondering, why in the world would they have left me in a running car. Back then I suppose it was not looked upon as being neglectful. And who would have figured I possessed the daredevil tendencies of Evil Knievel.

Another story she enjoyed telling was that of Tommy the rock thrower. I had a fondness for throwing them and apparently my favorite target was cars passing by on the street in front of the house. I apparently lacked accuracy, or the vehicles were traveling too fast because she didn't say anything about me hitting any. Busted just the same, I was caught in the act. Besides being a projectile thrower, my next best asset was being a runaway artist. When called down for my rock and roll tactics, I took flight, outrunning Mama. I was heading into the roadway until our neighbor, Cousin Charles Bowie ran me down and returned me to the scene of the crime. Mama, in both cases, cried as she delivered a spanking to me, tears rolling because she was thankful that I hadn't been hurt in a vehicular incident. Cars would play an ironic part in my unruly behavioral habits as I earned my license to literally test fate behind the wheel many years later. This is not the time to dish out that dirt though. Too many to include, many bullets dodged as well.

I have always had this renegade, rebel without a cause mantra. Why? Your guess is as good as mine. I yearned to be me and nobody else but me. I never wanted to be someone else or even like anyone else. I hated ever being compared to someone. When I say compare, I mean being compared for negative reasons. Please do not tell a kid you wish they were like somebody else or would do things like somebody else. These do not build character, confidence, or moral fiber. Most kids hate this motivational approach. I for one resented it and it would only serve to make me do the exact opposite. Maybe this led me to do a lot of the stuff I should never have considered doing. Pushing God and church on me ended with the same results. If I was pushed, I pushed back. I have said and I'll say it again. I believe in God. I never take his name in vain and I have nothing against church or those attending church.

My folks did not attend church regularly as I was growing up; hardly ever after I was a teenager. They did not force me to go, nor did they make me feel bad for not going. It was just a subject never discussed. There was no more of a Godly woman than my mama's mama, Ruby, my Granny Bowie. It concerned her that my folks did not attend church. Young Mary Bowie, my mama, had no choice while she lived under their roof. I seem to recall Mama saying something along those lines, that maybe she pushed back too. Once she was no longer under their roof, she spread her wings and exercised her independence. Possibly the apple does not fall far from the tree after all. She knew right from wrong, just like I know right from wrong. Making bad decisions when you know the difference does not justify the act. Live and learn and often the lesson is predictable, but we do it anyway, our way, the wrong way, the only way we see fit to do at the time. Good versus evil can be delightfully devilish to nonconforming daredevils. We stand out in the crowd, travel outside the clique, and do for all the wrong reasons because we can, or at least we think we are getting by without being caught. The thrill of the hunt prevails but believe me, they almost always come with consequences. Pay the price now or pay it later.

So, what have we learned in my latest psychobabble? I am not exactly sure. I suppose beginnings, if we are lucky, can have happy endings. Will mine be one of those fairytale stories happily 'everafters'? I can only stay the course and follow where it leads me. Cuz kick started this and I am sure he is doing what he can to see this through. My part is yet to be determined but I like where it is headed. No doubt, I am in a better place than I have ever been. I can only hope my chances are better than most. And as Paul Harvey might say…'and now for the rest of the story'.

If the truth be told, I was quite blessed growing up the only child in a small town, raised by parents who worked hard for everything they had. Working in a mill, in any capacity back then was not easy. My parents did well managing and stretching their earnings. Looking back, I can see that simple times were the best of times. My parents made sure that family spent times as family. They worked the second shift much of my young life, but both were awake before I headed off to school. We shared breakfast around the kitchen table because they would not be around at supper time during the workweek. It was important to them. I get it now. Mama was usually still at home when I arrived from school, but Daddy would already be at work. Less than an hour later she would join him. My black mama, Anise, would tag out and tend to me until midnight. She and I watched the first segment of Johnny Carson. When Mama arrived from work, we took Anise home and then waited at the mill for Daddy. I require extraordinarily little sleep to this day because of my early training and I was the only kid back then that knew all of Carson's characters and monologues.

Vacations were a special time each year, especially important to my parents. One to two weeks were set aside for the family bonding excursions. I saw much of the United States as a kid. Twice we took two-week road trips to California when backroads of America were the main routes traveled. The first time I was five but had my sixth birthday there while visiting an uncle and aunt I had never met. We visited Disney Land, Knotts Berry Farm and a movie set where they were filming my favorite television show, Circus Boy. I remember seeing my first ever lemon trees while there. I would be fifteen the next time we made the two-week trip coast to coast. Then we would take a northern route out there and southern route on the return. Along the way we would take in the touristy sights of Mount

23

Rushmore, the Badlands, the Painted Hills, Mount Zion Park, the Grand Canyon, Yellowstone Park, Las Vegas, Los Angles and Disneyland again, San Diego and world-famous zoo, and even walk across the border into Tijuana Mexico. On the way back we would stop at Tombstone Arizona, walk through Boot Hill, and attend an Atlanta Braves game at the Houston Astrodome. Blessed, just did not know it. Over the years I would see much of what this country had to offer from Key West to Niagara Falls and across the Canadian Border, my second country as a kid. We also visited Washington, DC, and a double header at Detroit Stadium. The boardwalk of Atlantic City, witnessing the diving horses on the Steele Pier and the singing group Freddie and the Dreamers entertaining on the pier as well.

My parents instilled in me the sense of adventure and urge to travel and see places I have never seen. As an adult I have continued that quest, visiting Branson, Missouri, many times, to Elvis's Graceland and his birthplace in Tupelo, Mississippi. New Orleans and Biloxi. I have retraced those trips to Key West and Niagara Falls. We even flew to San Fran with Cuz and his Judy then rented a car and drove up the west coast seeing God's wonderous redwood trees and that picturesque west coast. We even made a stop in Willow Creek in search of the illusive Sasquatch. We visited Lake Tahoe, and Reno a second time during the trip and Yellowstone and Grand Tetons a second time as well. We completed our journey flying out of Denver.

I digress, including this only to emphasize that I was not the product of a broken home, nor was I deprived much from a life of humble beginnings. My parents lived their life to the fullest. No, they did not attend church regularly, but they believed in the miracles of God and enjoyed viewing the world He created. I cannot blame my poorly chosen paths on them or on Him. How I lived most of my life is on me and nobody but me. Not bragging, no specific pride, it is what it is and no more. As I mentioned previously, I have made my fair share of reckless decisions and miraculously survived incidents I had no business surviving. No need excavating those ugly holes. Any family and friends still around are fully aware of the many mistakes in my perilous journey. Guess therefore I now wonder if the Man up

24

above had something in mind for me after all these years of near misses and miscalculated tragedies. No one to blame but the guy who stares back at me in the mirror.

No Push All Pull May 9, 2018

So much for my digressive ways. The past is history. I cannot change it or make it vanish. History, good or bad, is a lesson to be learned if indeed you are you have learned your lesson. For much of my life I made no apologies for who I am or anything I may have done. Saying you are sorry for what you did all those years ago does not amount to a hill of beans now. Most of those whom I might apologize to are no longer around today. Does this mean I have no regrets? A conscience can dictate the outcome. Sure, stupid decisions are always regretful especially if the outcome is equally tragic and idiotic. Let us return to the present and the dilemma I face coming to terms with what I am struggling to understand.

Today was a small step for many but a huge step for me. I conveyed this precise message to pastor Buddy Phillips, meeting with him to better understand this transformation I honestly believed was happening. I did not know how to begin. Buddy encouraged me to just tell my story, my way, on my terms, saying there was no right or wrong approach. So, I did. I explained my upbringing in the Pentecostal Holiness faith in a small church in Abbeville, South Carolina covering some key incidents that shaped my misguided resistance to the Godly path so to speak. He listened patiently as I changed gears, jumped about here and there, past, and present.

I am not one who likes to be pushed or takes kindly to having things pushed on me. The more you force something on me the more likely I am to push back. Don't tell me what I need to do, who I need to be more like or compare me to others and what they do and what I should do. I am me. I am not someone else. I am not supposed to be who you want me to be. I am who I am. Do not measure me by other people's standards. Push me. I push back. As explained, I believe in God. I have never taken the Lord's name in vain. I know the difference between right and wrong but that does not mean I haven't made my fair share of wrong decisions, many knowingly at the time. Does that make me a bad person, a terrible sinner, a forsaken soul? That is not for me to decide. Am I proud of everything I have done in my life? Certainly not, but something is changing in my life. I am trying to wrap my head around it, understand it and seek guidance for where I go from here. That is why this first meeting with Buddy is so critical.

I laid out the events that brought me to this crossroad in my life. My love for Sammy Cannon, the impact his death has taken on me and the doors opened by compiling a tribute book to My Brother, Sammy. The falling of those dominos, his death, Judy Cannon's journal and grieving process, the near miss accident, Buddy's sermon, and other factors contributing to the perfect storm. Buddy told me that I was no longer being pushed nor was I pushing back. I was being pulled. He explained that there was no timetable for what was happening. I had experienced no real relationship with God. He said that too much emphasis was put on the theological explanation for a relationship with the Lord. Everyone feels and deals with it differently, no right way or wrong way or single way to get there. This made me feel at ease.

I have joked with Buddy before and during this visit. He and I have traveled similar paths in our youths. We could probably have been best friends, partners in mischief if we had known one another as kids. He and I were both pranksters and daredevils. We exchanged a few more stories during this visit. What happens in a preacher's office stays in a preacher's office. Buddy has no choice. Sort of like a doctor, what I tell him should not be told to others. In my case, I can but only if I choose to do so. I am not sworn to secrecy. What I can share are stories that he shared, incidents that impacted his life. And I will when the time is right and I feel that can relate to my experience and to his. Most importantly is where do I go next.

As Buddy explained, first steps are to develop a spiritual routine in my life. I truly required guidance here because I had none. Buddy smiled as he shared his. First thing he does each morning as he exits his bedroom to the hallway is to ask God not to let him mess things up. The last thing he does as he enters his bedroom at night is to ask God to forgive him for things he messed up. He said each night he kneels beside his bed on his knees and prays. I stopped him there because if I got down on my knees it would be difficult for me to get back up. I explained that I have never been one to openly pray, especially in public. I do not volunteer praying, nor do I volunteer saying the blessing at a meal in public. I wave them off and pass them on to another. Buddy said there were no rules on praying out loud or in the public or even in kneeling at your bedside. He added that if ever I did want to though that he had some helpful tools to prepare me.

According to Buddy, I should develop a routine, suggesting that when I wake each morning that I spend about twenty minutes in meditation, reading scripture and so on. Lost in translation, how do I do this? He began tossing out reading Luke, John and Matthew and other stuff. I put on the brakes and asked him to write the stuff down. He obliged. He next suggested that prior to going to sleep each night that I pause, sit on the edge of the bed, and take a couple of minutes to pray. Me, pray. It could be about anybody, anything, no rules, and no specifics. Improvising is one of my skills, so it was going to be interesting to see where this took me. At least he gave me the option of sitting on the bed and not kneeling on my knees. Really, prayer can be done in any position; no rules for them either. He said for me to do what best suited me.

This meeting with Buddy was a wonderful first step. He said he looked forward to more when I was ready. Again, there was no schedule, just talk with him when I was ready. He added that he looked forward to my journey, heeding to the pull. We talked for an hour and a half. Not all was on God and me. We covered a ton of other subjects. Buddy made it easy for me to be me. I have always wanted to be me even when others felt I should be this way or that, like this person or another. When the dust settles, I am still me, for better or for worse, too old to change for the most part but not to old to learn.

Judy, my wife had written a sweet note to me and had left it by the coffee pot. She had prayed that my heart would some day be touched but had all but given up on it, especially when I pushed back on her attempts to guide me down this path. I had been quite abrupt at times. Push and I push back. It must happen when the time is right, the alignment of the stars or whatever. No, he took me there when

28

events were right for me to take note of the signs instead of kicking and screaming. Signs have been popping up quite frequently lately, so it seems. A bus had pulled out in front of me on my drive to the church to meet with Buddy. I was about to grumble about it when I read what was on the back of the bus. The catchy phrase jumped out at me, 'Follow and Believe'. Tell me if you think it is some sort of quirky message. It stayed in my lane all the way to my turn at the church. I shared this with Buddy, and he got a chuckle out of it.

Back to Judy. I shared how the meeting went with Buddy and what he said I should do. She gave me *The Message*, a modern translation for the Bible, given to her by her daughter Rhonda so, in the morning my next steps begin. Tonight, I step up my prayer game. This journey I feel is bringing us closer. She feels it too. We were having a few misunderstandings recently. I did make a stab at saying a prayer, but my prayer was for Sammy, God, or somebody to come to Judy in her dreams and fix her so things would be right. The joke was on me. It backfired and the fix was in for me instead. God does answer prayers even when prayed by a greenhorn. He fixes them the way He sees fit though and not necessarily when we think it needs fixing. Wish me luck. I am going where I have never gone before but, as Buddy explained, there is no timeline, no right or wrong way to get there. This is day one. Stay tuned. This should be an interesting ride.

Marking the Spot

I began my new routine last night and sat on the edge of the bed and prayed. Unlike any sporadic praying spells throughout my life, the focus was not directly on me per se. I am not sure if it is appropriate protocol to share what you prayed, so I will refrain from being specific. Let us just say I prayed for others that I knew were struggling or were faced with challenges that I was privy to and for those that we put our faith in to protect and do right for our great nation. Another baby step for me, but it was still a huge stride in the bigger scheme known as my new life moving forward. I am not sure where I am going by journaling this journey but for now let's just proclaim it is for me. Later, who knows? Possibly my approach, if successful and I am not doubting that it will not be, might help pave the way for others. As Buddy laid it out for me, no timetable, go at my own speed and take it as it pulls me. Thus far, mind and heart stay clear, open to what might come my way.

Furthering the routine, I did take time this morning to read some of the scripture from Mark as Buddy had mapped out for me. I am digesting that experience. It's new and I will be the first to admit that I'm certainly not there yet. I say this because merely reading does not translate to immediately understanding. There wasn't that wondrous 'ta dah' moment. I am not sure what I expected. I will just go with the pull for now. Perhaps reading it more than once might make it click, resonate in a manner that even I can grasp. One must remember this is a tremendous break through for me just walking down this path. There is no timetable. Everyone arrives at their own pace. I am 15 days shy of my 65th birthday. I am not expecting to miraculously turn this thing around in mere days or weeks. Never set the bar too high. It only promotes potential failure. I will take it as it comes, as it pulls.

I did download several books to my Kindle last night of *Daily Devotions, Walking Daily in New Testament and Proverbs and Lord Teach us to Pray, Coming to Jesus* and a fourth book, *Walking with God*. I figured it would not hurt having readily accessible reading material on my Kindle and smart phone. Before the Buddy meeting,

I had downloaded and begun reading chapters daily from Ted Dekker's *Waking Up To Whom You Really Are*. I figured reading anything spiritual couldn't be a bad thing. I am sure that my first rodeo will be filled with thrills and spills, many opportunities to climb back on that bucking bronco or pesky bull. Staying with the cowboy analogy, there is a new sheriff in town, and He will make sure I abide by the laws as written. Time to saddle up and see where this day takes me down what used to be a lonesome dusty trail. Today though, it is a much larger adventure, discovering previously unexplored territory. Head'um up, move'um out, yeeha. Move over pilgrim, we are heading to a range nearby.

Using a Mulligan

Okay, so my first attempt at reading scripture did not go as well as I had envisioned. I had my second 'official' prayer moment coming up. In my prayers prior to bed, I did as the night before, prayed for those that I knew were in peril, those who have challenges in their personal lives as well as those who faced potential medical issues. I did slip in one for me, help heal my aching back. After the Amen, I rested on my back for a while waiting for sleep to overtake me. During that time, I mentally talked to Sammy. I told him that he had gotten me into this, and he needed to help me with it. Where was Cuz, My Brother? He had not visited me in my dreams in months now. I willed him to visit me tonight. I even tossed out an invitation to God. Maybe I wasn't quite getting this whole process yet. It was new. I get that part, but I guess I was expecting more.

Off and on during the night I would wake up. Usually, I latch on to dreams and remember them vividly. Always have. I often use what I dream in my fiction writing. Each time I woke up I remembered nothing, very unusual for me. Where was Sammy? Where was God when I needed him? Don't take this the wrong way. I was not blaming Sammy or God, more tongue in cheek complaining. Still, I sought help in this new journey in the early stages. I guess I thought it would be a miraculous transformation or something. What do I really know? Newbies are just that and I am as green a horn that has ever existed for sure.

I glanced at the clock, 7:10, twenty minutes before my usual get up time. I turned back over, still having no dreams to hang my hopes on. I wasn't even thinking about Sammy, God or dreaming if the truth be known. I was just milking those last few minutes in bed. I must have drifted off. I woke fourteen minutes later. This time I remembered. I had had a dream. Like many dreams it did not make a whole lot of sense, nothing I could hang my hat on or so I thought. Sammy was not in it nor was God. Well, God in the Godliest of ways was not apparent. Let me paint the canvas, recap the dream.

I was on some sort of golf practice field with others. It became apparent it was associated with school. I was hitting balls, putting, and spending time with others that I did not recognize. For sure, Sammy was not there golfing with me. Next, I remember several of the guys mentioning that classes had begun. It then dawned on me that I had not checked in, so I rushed inside, not sure where I was headed. I located what appeared to be an administrative desk. A lady greeted me saying, 'Hello Tommy'. I told her I wasn't sure where I was supposed to be. She scribbled some information on a piece of paper and handed it to me. Puzzled, I shrugged. I still did not know where I was supposed to go. She motioned for me to follow her and she escorted me down a hallway and to a classroom. Inside was a male teacher sitting at a round table with one student, a boy that couldn't have been older than six or seven.

The teacher turned my way and said, "Hello. Why are you here?"

"What do you mean, why am I here?"

He became quite insistent saying, "No. Really. Why are you here? What's your story?"

I told him, "I retired in 2015. I am 65 years old. I married the first time when I was 18. I had a regular job at 18. That marriage lasted about two and half years. I married again. That one lasted 15 years. I am married now, been married for 23 years. I attended some classes in technical college, but I do not have a degree. I am here to learn. That's why I am here."

I then woke up. That was it. It was just a silly dream, no more, right? No Sammy, no God, no help. I was no closer to understanding the pull than yesterday and my scripture lesson was awaiting me, day two. My intent, I would just reread what I had read yesterday morning and hope something would click, something would resonate with me like it was supposed to do. That's how it's supposed to work, right?

I retrieved *The Message*, that Judy had given me. The paper Buddy had given me listing stuff to read was still marking the spot where I had read yesterday. I opened it and pages double folded over inside marked a new spot. I panicked. This was Judy's and I did not want to mess it up, so I unfolded the several pages and tried to hand iron out the wrinkles. While in the process of covering up my mess I noticed that I was at the introduction page to *The Message*. I began reading it instead of where I was supposed to go. My intent had been to read through Mark again, the sections named *John the Baptizer* and *God's Kingdom Is Here*. Instead, I was drawn to the introduction pages. Reading was reading, right. This was a little off plan though from what Buddy had suggested I do. No problem. I would skim through this first and then flip back to Mark. No harm. No foul. After all, Buddy had also said there was no right or wrong way to do this. So, I began reading.

It said that reading is the first thing, just reading the Bible. As we read, we are supposed to enter a new world of words and find ourselves in on a conversation in which God has the first and last words. Well, it must have. I certainly didn't. I did feel that I had been included in the conversation as it stated I should have been. Me, having a breakthrough was not going to come easy so it seemed. The Bible is not only written about us but to us, so it read. It went on to explain that we are used to reading books that explain things, or tell us what to do, or inspire or entertain us. That's a fact for sure.

God uses words to form and bless us, to teach and guide us, to forgive and save us. He draws us in by invitation and command to participate in His working life. We gradually or suddenly realize that we are insiders in the most significant action of our time as God establishes his grand rule of love and justice on this earth as it is in heaven. Revelation means that we are reading something we couldn't have guessed or figured out on our own. Okay, take a breath, so where does that land me in the scheme of things. I am obviously in that gradual category. No timetable so said Buddy. Maybe I am the one pushing this time and not relaxing and heeding to the pull.

It states that just reading the Bible, *The Message* and listening to what we read, is the first thing. There will be time enough to study later. Guess I was just reading and not really listening. I think this is going to require a serious paradigm shift for me. I am accustomed to reading. I am even accustomed to writing. Listening is a new concept. It says I am supposed to get a feel for the way these stories relate to me. When I am writing I become the characters and travel in their shoes, their ups and downs. I have got to open my mind and more importantly my heart.

The Bible does not introduce us to a nicer world, no predictable cause and effect. The Bible does not pretty up things and make the world a better place. Times were hard back then. Situations were tough. Lessons did not come easy, or without hardships. The biblical world is no perfect utopia, birds chirping, flowers blooming with forever joy. Step back and take another breath I tell myself. Nobody said this was going to be a walk in the park. It says that the Bible does not flatter us nor is it trying to sell us anything that promises to make life easier. Boy did I envision the wrong scenario. It is no escape from reality but a plunge into more reality.

I completed reading the intro and without going into further detail it opened my eyes more so than reading the passages in Mark yesterday. I could go on and on, quoting from it and relating to it but its best I leave some of this for you. I cannot teach anyone else because I am too new at this myself. What I can say is that God offered me a mulligan. Tomorrow I will tackle Mark again. This time I hope to be more open minded and learn from what I read in the intro. I asked for help and I got it. Those missed folded pages offered me guidance. Now it is up to me to take what I have learned and run with it. It is early yet in my journey. May the pull be with me. Prayers took a load off my back even if the pain in my back did not go away. Healing happens in different ways I suppose. Spiritual does not mean physical. God is not in this to fix my back. He is looking at the bigger picture, fixing me. I realize I have a long way to go, baby steps. Tomorrow is a new day. Cuz, it is partially your fault I am in the struggle to understand, thank you very much. Take that smile off your face. Remember, I am the one who managed your list so you would not forget or leave golf items at home. Love you My Brother. And a little help from you would not hurt. After all, you are up there close to the Man and all. I could use an angel about now.

As for that crazy late morning dream…I think I get it if it was indeed a message in a crazy sort of way. That teacher asked me, an old man in a child's class, why I was there. I answered by babbling about my past. I missed the point of the question. I was there to learn not digress. Learning starts by not only opening your mind but more importantly opening your heart. The learning curve has never been steeper and so unpredictably predictable. I arrived at that make believe school in my dream confused and unclear where I was supposed to be. Like now. I am uncertain and the uncertainty tends to cloud my thinking. Heed to the pull so said Paster Buddy. It is no more difficult than that. Old dogs struggle to learn new tricks.

Accidental Showman

Okay, I gave reading the scripture another try. I read the same one I had read two days ago. I am not sure if my role in this is the role of an interpreter or not but reading it this time some things jumped out at me just the same. Jesus is introduced and is traveling preaching the word. It seems at first that Jesus would rather play to smaller venues, be discreet in spreading God's word but touch those that needed to be touched, those needing God the worst. The cat escapes the bag though after he works the miracles with the vocal naysayer, the leper, and the cripple on the stretcher. He can no longer stay in the shadows and do God's bidding in a much smaller venue. His notoriety has put him in the center stage under the big top. The leper, even after asking him to keep it to himself, spews stories of this miracle worker. Now, my question is, was this mere accident or by design, God's will? Obviously reaching more people evangelistically should be a good approach, right? The more you can reach out to, convince, lead from sin cannot hurt.

One thing for sure is the fact that word of this Jesus character is spreading. He can do things no mere mortal man can. From childhood until now I have heard the stories of the leper and the person who could not walk. This theme has been played out over and over in books and movies even on the modern stage. Curing afflictions and saving lost souls is a good thing. God is good, right? It just seems to me that it quickly snowballed out of control and brought attention to Jesus, not only for good reasons but will eventually bring attention to those who will be out to get him before he becomes too powerful. There is no spoiler alert here. Unless you were born and stayed under a rock or are a nonbeliever you know the outcome of His notoriety.

I guess my question is, and I am not sure I should even be questioning it, is why Jesus didn't take the low road. Why God did not allow him to take the less obvious approach if for no other reason than to allow him more time to reach more people before the word became more widespread. A 'nobody' becomes a 'somebody' on the grandest scale. Then, those who are fearful of such power must extinguish the flame before it becomes an unstoppable firestorm. I am not questioning God's decision but just trying to understand the method to the madness per se on getting from square one to eventually Jesus being persecuted and nailed on that cross.

Lessons are supposed to be learned by reading the scripture. It is supposed to open your eyes and make you see things under a new light. Maybe I am not supposed to over analyze or try to take on the role of the interpreter. I cannot help it at this point, early in my journey as I read and try to understand. The mere fact that I am reading it, thinking about it, and typing this is another huge step for me in the baby steps I'm taking. I am almost obsessed with the urge to put what I think to writing, like I cannot wait to sit down in front of my laptop and put my thoughts down while they are still fresh. Bear with me and allow me some breathing room. As Buddy said, one must travel at one's own pace and in one's own way. It should not matter how we get there as long as we eventually arrive. I can honestly say that since this journey began, my fingers travel at lightening speed on my keyboard, intent on capturing the experience for me and who knows, maybe for others struggling as I have for so long with this subject, a relationship with God.

Changing gears, I did pray last night, and I did repeat my prayer for those I felt were suffering or needed a little extra help, including me. As I had done the night before, after my prayers, I laid there in bed rethinking things. It is not uncommon for me to have difficulty in going to sleep as my mind often races out of control. Sometimes I cannot seem to find the off switch to my brain. Again, I reached out to Sammy. No, I am not trying to reach him as one would try to reach out to God, but as an angel now and somewhat of a disciple of God. I have encouraged him to come to me and help me with this journey. As the night before, Cuz did not come to me. And, as the night before, I do not remember any dreams if I dreamed any. This is highly unusual for me, not remembering dreams or possibly not dreaming at all. If I take this as a sign, what sign must it be? Is this God's way of cleansing my mind better preparing me for what's ahead? I guess time will tell. For me, the journey continues. I cannot wait to see what's around the next corner or fork in the road traveled.

I am trying not to question it, to scrutinize it or read in things where things should not be read but it's all new for me. No, I am not unique or special in this process. I get that. But for 65 years I have not been part of it. I guess I need to relax and let the pull tug me at a pace meant for me. It is not how fast we arrive, right? The fact that I am even taking this journey is the bigger picture. Breathe in. Breathe out. Leave the driving to the designated driver. God, take the wheel and motor me to where I need to go next. One thing for sure, early in this process, I have been more aware of things going on around me. Signs, I seem to be more aware of the signs around me, convincing me that I am on the right path. My eyes are wide open, and my heart is opening to the prospects of transformation. Again, I cannot stress this enough, but my fingers blaze the keyboard like never before in all the years of writing books. I find it difficult to find a stopping point. In the bigger picture, I am not saying this is bad but at some point, I must stop. So, I will for the sake of carrying on in more normal daily activities. Don't touch that knob. Don't change that channel yet. I am sure there are blockbuster events ahead for me and those willing to open their minds and hearts and share what I am feeling, what I'm experiencing as my journey takes shape. Life is good. God is good.

Let's fast forward a tad, mid-morning, Judy and I having breakfast at Locals. Well, it is exactly as described, a local breakfast and lunch café on Seaboard Street in Myrtle Beach. Good food at excellent prices. While sitting there and attempting to carry on a normal conversation, my subconscious bounces around, thinking of the loss of Cuz. It is May now. He died in February. I continue to struggle with his death while I attempt to grasp my rebirth. Somehow the two are connected in my mind, more so than I can really wrap this little pea brain of my around. I believe that solving this mystery is the key to moving forward. Am I over thinking this process? There is no right or wrong way I remind myself. Nobody said it would be easy. It is early yet. Possibly I need to lower my expectations. During breakfast Judy receives a text.

The text is from Judy Cannon. My Judy just yesterday shared with her what I was experiencing and that I had credited Sammy's death with kick starting it. She had commented about how she felt positive that Sammy's death might have awoken me. It meant a lot to her as she continued to grieve her loss. In her text she told Judy that she had shared my experience with Lesli, Mandi and Kelli, Sammy's daughters; those of powers greater than us working miracles via Sammy's death. My journey continues. I feel it but the path is still unclear, masked with a bit of fog but I am making every effort to penetrate it. The pull moves at its own speed, not too fast for me to keep up with it but instead at a pace that I will not get lost along the way. I look forward to where this takes me. Baby steps…pushed and being pulled.

Doubling Down

Is it merely coincidence, maybe or maybe not? The scripture that I read this morning for my devotion so happened to be the exact same scripture Pastor Buddy read in church. Reading from Mark, it covered the tax collector and the Sabbath and how God dealt with the sinners. He embraced them on their grounds saying fixing them was more important than visiting with those already walking the straight and narrow. I got this from reading it and it was just reinforced when Buddy delivered it. After church as we departed to celebrate Mother's Day, I shook Buddy's hand as we exited. He told me he had read what I had written after our meeting a few days ago and congratulated me on some powerful writing about my experience.

Mother's Day, it is hard to believe that mine has been gone 14 years. She got her wings just three months prior to daddy getting his. She succumbed to pancreatic cancer and died in my arms while we both sat on the edge of her bed at home. Her last words before taking that last breath were, "I love you, Sweetie." Daddy died three month later while Judy and I fed him his Sunday meal, having been bedridden for nearly six years with Alzheimer and Parkinson. Aspiration got him before the paramedics could arrive. He died in that very same bedroom, their bedroom. He had been lying in his bed alert and watching as she took her last breath. My Granny Bowie, my mama's mom, would die in her bedroom after we moved to the Myrtle Beach from Abbeville. Chronic heart failure among other issues took her from us at the age of 93. My entire bloodline was gone in a matter of 11 months. Talk about a tough pill to swallow. I learned the meaning of depression.

I digress yet again, and I will probably digress even more before this journey ends. I have mentioned how Sammy Cannon's death set things in motion. I have also said how I have prayed and tried to get Sammy to help me, maybe visit me like he did directly after his death. Before I discuss the more current event, let me return to those three times Cuz did visit me. Dreams can be a form of visitation, portals for those who are no longer with us, so many believe. Sammy first came to me in a dream the morning of his death and two more times shortly their after. The dreams went like this…

Let me set up the first of the three. February 17 the phone rings, the call from Judy Cannon. I looked at the clock, 1:05 AM, commented to Judy this cannot be good. It wasn't. Sammy had lost his battle with leukemia. She and Mandi were by his side when he opened his eyes one last time and then just drifted away. We were numb and in shock. Eventually Judy drifted off to sleep sometime after 2 AM. I finally drifted off sometime after 4. That is when I saw Sammy one last time. It was so vivid.

His Judy, my Judy and I were sitting at a table. Sammy was across from us with his head resting on his arms face down. He raised his head and looked at us. It was not the old Sammy I was used to seeing. It was a much younger looking Sammy. He smiled. I stood and reached over, grabbing him by his arms, and placed my forehead against his. He was cool to the touch. He spoke, 'I love you my Brother.' He then said he was hungry. I retrieved what looked like a large plastic Easter egg and gave it to him. He opened it and it looked like an egg-shaped Reese's cup. Sammy popped it in his mouth in one bite and then said, 'I knew I could depend on you, my Brother.'

I then walked over to where Charles and Trudi Estes were standing by another table. Sitting at the Table were Janet Able Williams, Debbie Temple and another high school classmate, Judy Floyd who had also been battling cancer. I told them, "Sammy is here."

Trudi replied, "How can that be?"

Judy Floyd reached up and patted me on the arm. I leaned over and caressed her shoulder and kissed her on top of her head. I then walked to another table where Jerry and Norma Solomon were sitting. I told them, 'Sammy is here.'

Norma said, 'He can't be. The Doctor pronounced him dead.'

I said, 'No, he's here.'

She asked, 'Where?'

I pointed to two oversized wooden swinging doors and then said, 'He went in there, to the bathroom.'

I then woke up. Maybe those enormous wooden doors weren't the bathroom after all, and My Brother visited me to say a final goodbye before completing his journey.

Here is the second dream, visit as I call them. April 12, 2018, Cuz just will not let me be, thank you very much, My Brother. He continues to dog me, fueling more entries for the original tribute book. He has this uncanny way of reaching out to me from his world to my dream state.

Let me frame this dream. We are at some sort of beach cottage. Sammy's daughters are there. All sorts of activities are going on. Out of the blue Cuz arrives. I spot him standing in a doorway with Mandi, the middle daughter, by his side, her arm looped in his. He is red faced, not unusual to see him with a flushed face. I walk over to him and tell him, 'I don't want to go.'

He smiles and says, 'Then don't.'

I touch his face with the back of my hand and then wake one minute before the alarm is set to sound, my wakeup call to start another workday. Having retired at the end of 2015, I only work part time, one week a month and only set that clock radio during my work weeks. It is funny how that brief encounter with him was so vivid, can stick in your head and seem so significant. Penning that tribute book and the journey of a life that is good seemingly never ends. My Brother still has this unique and uncanny way of tossing his two cents in when you least expect it. Loving it, love him. I will take every snippet offered. Dreams, memories, forgotten stories, are all good. Life is good, right Cuzy. You lived it to the fullest. And as Sinatra would belt out, 'You did it your way.' I so look forward to more of your spontaneous visits. If need be, we will leave the light on for you in Suite 101, not that you really require those human creature comforts now. He always referred to the guest bedroom as Suite 101. I babble. I do so because I have this urge to milk and cherish this precious moment. Like everyone else who loved you, it is a constant struggle for me believing that you are actually gone, that I will never hear 'Cuz' echoing in the background and wondering what the heck you want now.

Dream number three, April 17, 2018. While still compiling my tribute book to him things just happen. I am not sure why, but I feel compelled to share them as they do. I do not pretend to understand them but to me they seem significant. Here goes yet another, the third in the brotherly visits as I have come to name them. In the dream…

I walk with Sammy from a house to some sort of shed. He is piddling. He has always been good at piddling. I do not ask him what he's doing but I do ask him how he's feeling. He smiled and said, 'I'm feeling great. There was a time when I wasn't. They stopped pumping that stuff in me and now look at me, not even a nose drip. I'm going to make it Cuzy.'

That was it. You be the judge what it meant. It's late in the morning and I keep drifting in and out of sleep, looking over at the clock what seems every couple of minutes or so. Next little dream snippet, I am with Janet Holmes, another cousin explaining to her the importance of keeping a journal, The Janet Journal. She laughs, says, 'You mean a diary. Mom started one for me, made the first entry.' Janet is very much alive and living in Georgia. I have not seen her in many years. Her mom has been long passed. She was the sister-in-law to my Granny Bowie.

I wake and look at the clock again; only two more minutes have passed. I nod back off. Next, I see Judy Cannon in another vivid dream. She says, 'The cancer is real.' I wake for good this time, one minute past my normal get up time. That one-minute thing again. Before it was a minute early, now a minute past. What does it mean? The journey never ends. All is good even if I do not quite comprehend it.

As the commercial goes, 'But Wait!' Shortly after I get up, I go through my morning motions, including quickly perusing Facebook. There, the third entry is a statement that reads, 'Look, I can bowl sometimes. I just bowled a 255. Hope I can keep this up three games next time.' The entry was by my cousin, Janet Holmes, not to me, just a general comment.

You tell me. What are the odds of this happening? Did My Brother pull off some sort of crazy connection to another one of my cousins? And if he did, what the heck does it mean? Significant or not, the experience made me feel good. Will there be others before this tribute book to Cuz is completed? Don't ask me. I am not the one in control. You cannot make this stuff to happen. Greater powers are in the driver's seat. That's what my gut tells me.

Back to now and me being caught in the pull. I have been trying to encourage Cuz to help me on this journey, possibly in a dream if you can make such a request come true. Like I have said, I have given him much of the credit for me being where I am right now, his death kick starting the process. Well, like I have done over the last few nights, I have asked God and Sammy for help. Well, either Sammy decided to do something about it, or God used him as a tool. Either way, it happened last night. It has been months since I had that last dream about Sammy. As previously disclosed, I had not dreamed the last couple of nights, or I did not remember dreaming if I did, both highly unusual for me.

I woke to Judy's cell phone alert message and glanced over at the clock, 1:48. I had only been in bed about an hour and a half. She slept through the whimsical alert. It was at that moment that I realized I had been dreaming. Lying there thinking about it, the dream came into focus. It was about Sammy. Watch what you wish or pray for is all I am saying. Cuz was in a hospital gown sitting in his recliner. My Judy and his Judy were there. I was doing what I usually did with Cuz, joking and messing around with him. I tossed something over at him, not sure what, but it struck him on his belly, and he screamed in pain, yelling, 'Dang it, Cuz.' I was embarrassed by my actions, apologized, and began crying, saying I was going to leave before I did more harm. Next thing, he is coming back in the room wearing some sort of armored protection and carrying a long pole with a boxing glove attached to the end, laughing, he was ready for me now. I jabbed my hand at the boxing glove and remained there with him.

I woke next and it was after 4 AM. After a visit to the bathroom and briefly reflecting about the dream, I dozed back off. About an hour later I woke a second time, this time very distraught and aware I had been visited a second time by Sammy. This time we were near a lake or pond, Cuz, the two Judy's and I. Sammy was perched on the bank, still wearing that hospital gown, oxygen tube running to his nose. He appeared to be resting. I decided to take a walk and encircled the body of water. When I returned, Sammy was gone. So was his Judy. I searched frantically for them, finally finding my Judy and his. His Judy asked me where Sammy was and all I could say was that I could not find him. He was gone and I feared the worse given where I had last seen him. This was awful. This was not how I wanted a visit to happen. After searching and searching I returned to a room and found him in bed with his eyes closed. Before I could check on him, I woke up. I was extremely troubled by both dreams.

I have thought a lot about those dreams, his visit, today. Was there a purpose, a lesson to be learned? Thinking about the scripture from Mark, this is my take on it. God wanted to spend more time with the sinners and did not need to spend time with those who no longer needed Him. Just maybe, Sammy came to me and then left just as quickly because he no longer needed God to help him through his perils, but I did. It could have been Sammy's way, with God's help of pointing out to me that I no longer needed him, that he would be simply fine, that I was the one searching right now, somewhat lost but trying to find my way. He showed me he had been in pain but quickly was pain free now. He then in his way showed me that he was lost but had been found. I don't know. I am trying to figure out things and sort through the signs. My takeaway though is just maybe I do not need to call on Sammy anymore. He has shown me the way. Just keep following the pull. Everything will be all right. I love and miss you Cuz.

Satan Versus Satan

My biggest challenge and it has nothing to do with battling Satan. I am retired, have been for 2 ½ years. I still work one week a month for my employer and today begins my first work week since this journey has commenced. What does that mean for me and my time of reading the scripture and the challenges of understanding them? I am rising before 6 AM leaving me little time to read. I might have to come up with a plan B, possibly change my time to night or afternoon meditation. This morning though I will read an abbreviated version, Satan versus Satan from Mark. Jesus must fend off those who are accusing him of performing black magic. He pushes back on this premise though. He explains to his accusers that it makes absolutely no sense to think this way. He warns them that they are taunting the one that would forgive them for their sins. He helps and heals people and they just do not get it.

Dream state wise last night, there was no Sammy. That is okay. I think the previous night he made it clear that I no longer needed him as a Cuz crutch. I did dream and I think most were screwy nonsensical dreams. I say I think because I do not remember them too well. That trend continues. I am trying to rationalize if the pull has some odd impact on my dreaming. Not sure and, if it does, what does it mean? I am grabbing at straws I'm sure, making something out of nothing, trying to draw a correlation. Still, dreams have been a big part of my life. I tap into them for writing material. Odd how I am now documenting my journey effortlessly. My ideas are coming from my inner self and have been influenced by the pull, so it seems. I am not saying that is bad, simply different. God is controlling the keyboard for now. I still think about My Brother though. I wonder if that pain will ever completely go away. Time heals all so they say. Tomorrow is another day. Another day without my brother, Sammy Cannon.

Sitting on a Bag of Seed

During my designated work week, more times than not, I usually wake before the radio alarm signals it is time for me to rise and shine. Not this morning though. I slept until it rudely woke me. I thought since I had been startled from slumber that it explained why I for the first time in several mornings vividly remembered my dream, at least the one I was experiencing at my wake-up call. I shall recap it because at it turns out has significance in my start to a new day. I caution patience though. This will be a long-winded lesson of sorts, and just after I questioned why I wasn't remembering my dreams lately, go figure.

The dream as best I can remember from its beginning has me and a friend, a coworker from the "way back' time commuting to work, me riding with Gene Walker. For the record, Gene was a coworker from my working days at Flexible Technologies in Abbeville. I put in 19 ½ years there. Gene was a black associate that died while I was there, an illness brought on by kidney failure. We are talking over thirty years ago. I must clarify for record. I have never dreamed about Gene before. For whatever the reason I was hitching a ride with him to work, something that never happened in real life, so why now? On our way Gene decides to stop by a dilapidated and tiny travel trailer parked on the edge of the woods near a steep sloping hill. Neither of us knows the family, which includes a dad, mom and three or four children, all white, not that it matters but just framing the scene. Gene mentions rain is coming and that we need to help them better prepare for it, the travel trailer not in the best condition to weather a storm. Weathering a storm, how profound is it that I am typing that phrase.

From somewhere we locate a huge clear plastic tarp. Gene and I began affixing it so that it will protect the trailer from the rain. In the dream I am complaining a bit, saying we do not know these people and we're going to be late for work. Gene just smiles and goes about his business, implying nothing matters but the task at hand. I stop my whining and help. We eventually finish but the bottom of the tarp is free flapping in the wind, and we have nothing to secure it. We had done the best we could with what we had to work with. We spend a few minutes getting acquainted with the family. The parents offer us warm thanks. Next scene in the dream, we are at Flexible. I see a mixture of characters there, some from my past at Flexible; some from other places I have worked and a few from where I currently work. You know how dreams can be scrambled like this.

I spot a fenced in section with wood leaning against the outside. It is scrap wood, perfect for securing the bottom of that tarp. Upon closer observation I spot a pallet of books locked inside, my books, books I have written. A lady is standing nearby. I tell her I need access to those books to take home. I ask her about the wood. She tells me to help myself and unlocks the gate to the cage. Utilizing a pallet jack, I pull the books and relocate them off the aisle near the front entrance and the time clock. I then return to retrieve the wood just as the horn sounds that the shift has ended. I have this uncanny ability to recall my dreams or I had before I fell under the influence of the pull.

Wood in hand, I return to the front entrance and spot my books spilled into the aisle. I am furious. Some coworkers are near the timeclock. As I begin gathering up my books, I notice that at least half are missing, maybe twenty or more books. Ron Beers, another coworker, this one from Metglas in Conway, tells me that various employees were snatching up copies as they punched out. He identifies several of them. I am livid, angered by this horde of book thieves. I am waiting for Gene to arrive while picking up the remaining books and placing them back on the pallet.

Where is Gene? I don't need him lollygagging right now. Patience is not one of my virtues. I storm off and head to the front office to file a grievance and ask them to check their security camera, the one located above the timeclock, to identify the culprits. As I am walking there, I begin thinking how I am going to explain why I have all these books inside the facility. Soliciting is a cardinal rule at the company. In my defense I will tell them I was not openly soliciting them, just had them there in case anyone asked me about wanting one. I realize that will not fly, even in my wildest dreams. Dreams…right.

I detour and head back to where my books are supposed to be, thinking that I should not have left them unguarded. More might be gone. It then dawns on me. Just possibly I am wrongly accusing these folks. Because the books were conveniently located by the timeclock and exit, just perhaps people thought they were there as giveaways. Maybe I should not be so quick to blame and judge. The radio blasted abruptly ending my dream. I began my morning ritual of preparing for my parttime workday, latching onto the dream, simply happy I was back to remembering them. I had just enough time to squeeze in a quick scripture.

Still in Mark, I began where I left off yesterday morning, The *Sewing of the Seeds* story. Most know how this goes. I even remembered it from church sermons, or it being read to me as a kid in Sunday school. I had never read it myself though, not until now. Sad to admit this as a nearly 65-year-old-man but it is what it is. Jesus tells the story of the seed being flung about to those gathered around to hear his teachings. Jesus is in a boat just offshore because the crowd is so large. He explains how the seed falls in various places, like in cracks, hardened soil and in the weeds. He then teaches why in each case it fails to germinate. Then, some falls on fertile soil and flourishes. The lesson he teaches is that like the seed, to flourish and grow, you must open your heart, learn to forgive, and share with others. Do I need say more? The irony, I am again remembering my first vivid dream in a while if you discount the Sammy one from yesterday. This one links to a scripture that I eventually read afterwards. Coincidence, I don't think so. I believe the pull is becoming stronger. Of course, this is my story, and I am sticking to it. Live and learn. God is Good, right Cuz?

Okay, now it is time for me to quickly digress. Just prior to my retiring last night, as I plugged my cell phone into the recharger, I noticed that I had a text message. Having worked today, I had muted my cell phone and had not taken it off mute. The text was from Judy Cannon and it pertained to Sammy. The text read as follows from Lesli (Sammy's daughter) to Judy and it is about Jackson, Lesli's youngest son, too young to articulate memories about his Poppy, Sammy, or so we thought. Braeden, the older son plays indirectly into it too.

The text from Lesli reads…

"We were in the car on the way home and Jackson was in the back seat just talking and laughing. Braeden and I thought he was talking to himself. Suddenly, he says, 'Poppy, you love me all the way from Heaven? Good, I love you all the way from *earf*.' So precious. Out of the mouths of babes."

Sammy, I am sure with a little elbowing by God, still has this knack for reaching out where it is needed, even three months after he earned his wings. In this case, possibly the younger grandchildren are being impacted by the pull. Sow those seeds while it is prime planting time. Boy, what a day so far and I have only been up less than thirty minutes. Hi-ho, hi-ho, it's off to work I go. Life is Good as is God who created it.

Life's lessons continued to resonate with me after I arrived at work. I engaged in two separate discussions during the morning hours while there. The first was with a supervisor, Jimmy, agonizing over doing performance evaluations with several of his employees. He was stressing about having to discuss some negative behavior. One employee had made several mistakes recently because she had rushed to complete the tasks at hand. I listened to the incidents and offered some friendly advice. I suggested that why not ask her why she felt compelled to rush through her tasks and take shortcuts. Could it be that she felt others were not pulling their fair share of the load and she was compensating, or maybe she thought she had a quicker way, a better solution for completing them? If so, he could use it as constructive interaction to come up with a solution. He was obviously very distraught over her and a couple others' performances. I suggested that first he should build on some positive things they were doing and then point out where they could do better in some of the situations that were problematic for him. Cultivate a few seeds in fertile ground so to speak. See, I am grasping and learning from the pull.

The second situation was with an employee, a friend, Dwayne, that had suffered a lost time accident. He had dropped by to say hello. I asked him how the injury was going, and he caught me up to speed. This was a very lengthy discussion. He is black and we talked about cultural differences, our takes on the black versus white thing. I shared many examples throughout my life that pointed out how I felt I was colorblind to these differences. I began by explaining how I had been raised by my black mama from a young age until I reached teenage because both my parents worked the second shift. It was enlightening and rewarding talk from both of our perspectives, too long to cover here. Dwayne then explained that he was a bit aggravated because he felt he was being underutilized resulting from the lost time injury status. I asked him if his medical situation did not improve, just what he wanted to do in life, if not here, elsewhere. As a mere fifty-two-year-old, he had a long way to go and could be faced with potential disability status or challenges to return to his regular job within the facility. I suggested that why not go to the Human Resources Director and lay out a case that he would like to play a more intricate part in the workforce, a more beneficial role for the company. He had suffered what he considered some prejudices over the years, unfairly turned down for positions in the company because of his color, much with the previous HR leader. That still stuck in his craw.

Try this I encouraged him. Go to the current HR person, explain how you don't want to just report to work every day and rely on the company finding slug work, grunt jobs to just keep you in line to receive a paycheck. While having to be on light or restricted work duty, you want to step up to the plate. Forgive and forget what happened in the past and look to the future and how you can help. Learn to forgive. I was planting seeds once again. Boy how a short devotion this morning has made me see the light within the pull. I guess this thing is starting to click or at least I am experiencing breakthroughs along the way.

Pastor Buddy might just beam a bit too the next time we meet. He told me he would not schedule another meeting, that I would know when the time was right. Now it does not mean that either of these coworkers will heed my advice, but at least I tried to offer alternatives to their precarious situations. I am far from being an expert but being a messenger is just as important in the big scheme of things. All I can say is that I feel good about today and what I was able to do, how I approached the scenarios as they dropped in my lap. Everything happens for a purpose, right? It started with that crazy dream and then the brief reading this morning from Mark and sewing those seeds. Funny how things can snowball when you least seem aware of the avalanche approaching. Journaling the journey from push to pull continues, coming to a venue near you possibly. God is Good.

Symbolic Interpretation

Dreamland tended to be a bit quiet last night. I have no vivid recollection of any that I might use in my lessons learned or in future fiction writing. Sammy was MIA, again, too, and that is okay. I think or at least I hope I am beyond needing him to push me further into the pull. The pull seems to be functioning simply fine for now. I woke before the alarm. That left me a few extra minutes of wiggle room to read where I left off yesterday morning, still in Mark. I am typically a slow reader under the best circumstances but reading Biblical stuff is not like reading a novel. Extra sponging is required to absorb the intent of the scripture. See, I do get it. Even a Newbie has his moments. Pastor Buddy said to take time after I got up for morning meditation. I'm not sure that my approach to this would qualify as genuine meditation but I'm doing the best that I can, no right or wrong way, slow boating it. I would say I am still knocking off the rust, but that would imply I am rusty. Obviously, I am not. I qualify more as brand new in the scheme of things.

In this morning's devotion Jesus is still working his miracles out and about the lake. He encourages those being wowed to join him in the boats and travel to the other side. During their journey, an ugly storm comes up, waves threatening to capsize the boat Jesus is in, terrifying those aboard. Jesus is peacefully sleeping, oblivious to the turbulence around him. They panic and wake him. Soon after the storm subsides and the waters calm. They eventually make it to the other side. Many encounters greet Jesus and his ever growing crowd of thrill seekers.

Jesus first encounters a wild and crazy madman from the cemetery named Mob. No chains or ropes can contain him. He is a force to be reckoned with and most of them are terrified of Him and His rioting ways. He has no use for Jesus or any of the others. Not to worry though, Jesus transforms him, cured him from his torment, and reformed him as a believer. He wants to go where Jesus goes but Jesus insists, he go his way and tell his story of what happened. He abides and preaches the teachings. Next Jesus encounters a woman who has been hemorrhaging for a dozen years, no one able to stop the bleeding or cure her. She takes the backdoor approach to the healing process by covertly placing her hand on the robe of Jesus.

You can run but you cannot hide. He senses the touch and calls out the one who has touched his garment. She eventually takes responsibility for her action. There is no punishment for her, just acknowledgment. Then, there is the child that is supposedly inside her parents' home, lifeless, presumed dead. How can Jesus cure the dead? Impossible most proclaim. The twelve-year-old girl is released from what holds her motionless and yet another miracle has seen the light of day.

These were powerful revelations brought on by Jesus, the man in charge with the power to cure and transform what needed to be. That's my take. So, what am I to learn from this? What ahead in my day will intertwine with this scripture to make it more meaningful in my life? Those are fair questions. I don't have a dream to hang a hat on or to draw correlation. Am I going to encounter a madman at work, interact with a lady in distress or cross paths with a child in need? Time will tell I suppose. My peripheral vision remains on high alert. Most of these relative teachings have blindsided me. I never saw them coming until I was slap dab in the middle of them. Why should this morning be any different? As I shower, an understanding begins formulating in this little pea brain of mine.

As the spray of hot water rejuvenates me for the day ahead, I realize that everything I just read relates to me, plain and simple. Just hear me out. The madman represents me, roaming wildly throughout life, ranting and out of control, no chains or ropes capable of restraining me from how I choose to live my life, all for fun, loyal to none. Possibly a little over exaggerated but you get the point. My past was not always pretty, plenty of highs and lows for sure.

Second lesson learned as it pertains to me was that of the woman, bleeding and suffering, no cure in sight. How can I relate to her? My life up until now has been incurable, bleeding but surviving, accepting who I am, take who I am or not, it is your problem, not mine. I just ignore it and move forward, doing the best I can under the situation I cannot control nor have the will to change. I cannot change nor stop the bleeding. I stopped trying a long time ago if ever I even attempted to stop it. A cure always existed if I had taken time to look for it. Now, I am not saying I am perfectly cured yet, but I am in the beginning stages of healing hopefully. I did not openly look for it. I did not raise my hand and shout pick me, Lord. Fix me.

Make me better. It snuck in a little tug when I was not looking, maybe hoping I would not notice. I noticed as He knew I would eventually notice. Let's just leave it at that.

Finally, there is that lifeless child, thought to be dead and beyond hope or help. That is me too, possibly the easiest analogy to make sense of. I have been dead for nearly sixty-five years, lifeless for all practical purposes. I'm not going to be so bold as to proclaim I have been reborn just yet, but I have awoken, and I am breathing again. Where there was once no hope, there is now. Judy told me she had given up hope that I would ever find Christ. She had prayed until she was blue in the face, and had finally just decided she had to accept me for who I am. Her solution, she would work on herself to find peace and just make the best of it. Surprise, the sleeping child has been jolted from a Rip Van Winkle like state. First, I must learn to breathe on my own and then the rest should eventually fall in place. Sounds easy but no journey is without stumbles and falls and poorly chosen forks in the road. Guess I must depend on my GPS, God's Powerful Support.

Crazy as it sounds and I do keep beating this dead horse a bit, but my fingers move at lightning speed on the keyboard as I journal this journey. I put thought into my fiction writing, weighing out the scenes, developing the characters and scenarios but this is entirely different. My brain is processing what my fingers are typing at a speed I am not accustomed to. How does that country song go? Jesus take the wheel or something like that. It defies explanation, so I will just go with it and stop trying to explain it. So begins another day in the shadow of the pull. The leering question, will my interpretation stand or will other events in the day mesh with what I read? I suppose if nothing else develops, I have come to terms with the scripture as I perceive it relates to me. That is mighty powerful given my journey in life up until now. Cuz, I hope you are paying attention and are proud of my progress thus far. You trusted and believed in God until the very end. My Brother, you were indeed an inspiration.

An incident occurred at work shortly after I arrived. A supervisor went off on the director of operations. My cubicle is located just a few short paces from his office. The supervisor was livid, loud, and shouting obscenities, obviously not pleased with a recent incident. I have never heard this individual shout and curse like this. I stayed clear of the situation. Later, while I was outside conducting a follow-up audit of the plant grounds, ironically I crossed paths with the supervisor. I greeted him and then asked if he was okay, that I had never heard him display so much anger. He told me that he usually does not let things rattle his cage and if something does, he takes time to pray about it until he calms down enough to discuss the matter. Today he fell off that wagon and allowed his emotions to get the best of him. He said that he did his praying this time afterward and asked God for forgiveness. He then returned to his boss's office and apologized for his unprofessional outburst. He told me that the incident had happened because he did not take kindly to being accused of being a liar and a thief. I told him none of this was any of my business, but I congratulated him on the path he had taken to make things right with the Lord and with his boss.

There was a time when I would not have appreciated the gravity of this conversation, the God forgiving part. There is never a wrong time to ask for forgiveness and say that you are sorry. The pull never lets an opportunity slip by without taking time to introduce a lesson plan. We are all human. None of us are perfect and we will always make mistakes. The key is to learn from those mistakes, reconcile them and stay on course for the greater good. This is way too profound for me. Undoing sixty-five years is going to be a bumpy ride and an incredible journey indeed.

Update from yesterday. Friend Dwayne stopped by and said he had followed up on what we had discussed. He had gone to talk to the HR Director, but he was out of the plant until next week. He marked it on his calendar to follow up next week and thanked me for the advice. I wished him the best in pursuing his goals.

Identity Crisis

My morning devotion was abbreviated because of my work week. Still in Mark, I read 'Just a Carpenter', the marching orders for the twelve and the feeding of five thousand. I remembered two out of three, the feeding the five thousand one. I am not sure why I feel compelled to always quantify if I dreamed and if I remember the dream and if it plays part in my journey. Whatever the reason, my dreams have been playing an intricate part, not every morning but more mornings than not. It dawned on me that no dreams were really jumping out at me this morning. I began wondering if because of the pull, my dreams were becoming less important in my life. Let me try to explain.

I have always had a vivid imagination. Maybe it's from being an only child and living in a make-believe world became a powerful tool for me growing up. Possibly this imaginary world carried over into my dream state and that's why I have always had vivid memories of them when I wake up. Pure speculation on my part but I am just trying to understand why I am now struggling more so than ever to remember them on a regular basis. This has never been a serious issue before, not that I take dreams seriously, other than the visits from those we have lost. I guess I am just noticing a difference. Could it be that my heart is being lifted, a burden being removed and that dreams are no longer my somewhat escape pod from reality? Or maybe I am just over thinking stuff, reading something into something that in the big scheme of things doesn't really matter. Hey, like I have said, some of my best writing material has come from dreams. Possibly I am in denial and in somewhat of a distraught state facing the consequences of losing a major conduit for writing subject matter. Okay, enough of this, let us move on to this morning' scripture and decipher the lesson hopefully learned.

Jesus was a carpenter before he became famous for working miracles and inspiring the uninspired. Fame does not necessarily bring fortune. Some say it is tough to go back home when you have reached a certain status. The followers, good and evil, see him one way while family still see him as a mere mortal, a carpenter, nothing special at all. Your parents sometimes still see you as their child and overlook that you are now grown and have secured your place as an adult. This lesson haunts me. I can relate on so many levels. It's that thing, me just wanting to be me part of my life. Parents can be unintentionally cruel and unaware of their impact. Often, they think they are helpful when instead they are harmful. As children, we are often molded and shaped as they wish us to be and it prevents us from having the chance to become us. Being carpenter by trade does not mean that you want to spend your life being a carpenter. Aspiring to be more or be something different can adversely be impacted by those seeing you as only they wish to see you. Jesus did wonderful things outside his home life but when he returned to family, it was easy for them to see him as that boy or just a carpenter. We often see ourselves differently than family.

My mom had a bad habit of comparing me to others when I was a kid. She often pointed out what cousins were doing and how I should be more like them or do what they were doing. I don't think this was meant to be harmful, but I took exception to it. I was me. I wanted to just be me and for them to accept me as me. I had no desire to be somebody else. I wanted to find my own way and do what interested me. I was not stupid nor was I an overachiever. I pushed forward at my own speed staying in the middle of the road in my comfort zone. As I had explained to Pastor Buddy, push me and I push back. The mold was set at an early age. I was a rebel without much of a cause, even before I understood the concept. I fought hard to just be me but as I got older, I was losing the battle. So, what did I do? I became someone else and not the person I wanted to be, nor the person others wanted me to be. I guess you could say I mutated into something else. My rebellious ways became quite costly, sometimes downright dangerous, and self destructive.

Unlike Jesus, He knew who He was and who He wanted to be and had discovered purpose in His life. I was still searching and evolving into something else. My objective, I was not going to fit the mold. I was going to be the furthest thing from it. This would lead me down a self-destructive path much of my life, an unorthodox way of gaining attention, mostly for the wrong reasons. Just hang in there with me. I am learning as I go and telling it as I now see it, looking back and figuring it out. As Pastor Buddy told me; I must travel at my own pace. The key is that I learn and heed the pull. On that premise, I continue. I can't help nor hinder the process, from my brain to my fingertips on the keyboard. It's just a process under Greater guidance. To understand the journey, I must first understand myself. I must explore where I started, what went wrong and how I got here. How do you fix sixty-five years of doing what you thought you wanted to do? Answer, you cannot fix or undo what has already been done.

I developed a defense system and I enhanced it as I grew older. Wit, sarcasm, and rebellious tactics became an intricate part of my arsenal. Like any comic, I became quick with one-liners, comebacks, putdowns and rubbing it in when I saw how it impacted those under assault. Everyone was fair game. And like any true comedian, I did not laugh at my own jokes. Instead, I developed a poker face. Eventually I was not laughing at others' jokes. I kept my emotions in tack and for the most part, concealed within. I became quite proficient at it; too good some might say.

Not only was I resistant to becoming what others wanted me to be, I lost all concept of me, who I had wanted to be. I sort of flipped and ventured over to the dark side. No, I was not a Satan worshipper or anything like that. I always believed in God, but I just ventured down darker paths, made bad decisions, and seemed to always be trying to prove myself as being the daredevil, the one who did not care and the type of person that would push the envelope to draw attention from my peers. I was the good kid gone bad so to speak. Pushing back morphed into pushing the envelope as far as I dared take it. Reckless behavior became the norm. I had several near misses, any of which could have brought a tragic ending to my rebellious ways. Given how I dodged tragedy, did God have a greater purpose in mind for me or was He just not giving up hope for me? Sixty-five years is a long time to stay the course of what some might see as a lost cause.

Jesus transformed from a mere carpenter to the Messiah. No, I am not in any way comparing myself to that status but what I am trying to understand is look where I was and the journey I have taken to get here, right now. In or around 2003 writing became my escape. I say that now, but I did not really see it then. Two failed marriages, too many bumps in the road and an assortment of bad baggage along the way had made for a worse than imperfect life. My dad was suffering from Alzheimer's and Parkinson. I was commuting from

Greenwood, South Carolina to Commerce, Georgia every week and staying there three days while working there. I began writing my first so called novel while staying in a hotel and used it as more or less just something to do. As it turned out, looking back now, it was an escape for me from reality. Using my wild and crazy imagination I could become the hero, the villain, or any assortment of characters within the content and pages.

Losing both parents and my grandmother in an eleven month stretch pushed me more so into my writing. It was an escape. I pushed back on being the 'me' that had to deal with all this death and could be a character within my fictional stories. I was still searching for my own identity. I wanted to be me in the worst way, but I no longer knew who 'me' was. Ironically, I had become this character that I had developed, just like a character in a story. Mom had always wanted me to be something I was not back then and now others still wanted me to be different than the person I had become. I was still pushing back. Just accept me for who I am, who I have been for the last sixty-five years. I cannot change. I am who I am or so that was my lame story. I did not want to change. Why after all these years must I change? Push. I push back, just that simple. I rebel. I turn it up a notch just to prove my point. It was my ultimate defense mechanism. I was no carpenter, and I was not me either.

Fast forward. Writing became an outlet for me, therapy so to speak. I completed that very first sloppy novel and leapt into the next and then the next. *The Caregiver's Son, Outside the Window Looking In*, was my first real attempt at writing about me and my experiences. At the time it was just for me. Years later I allowed Judy to read it. She said it might help others dealing with the caregiving process. This was after several of my fiction books had been published. In writing, not only did I find a release I also discovered that by writing, I could be me. I was finding something that brought me joy, gratification, and a place in the world. I became an author. I chose to become an author. Through this experience I connected with readers and other authors. Like Jesus coming back home, family does not always embrace the concept. Allow me to explain. Friends and family are eager to buy your work the first couple of times. As you write and publish more though, they try not to make eye contact with you, avoiding having to buy another book. I say this in good fun.

Writing did allow me to fill a void, to reinvent myself under the persona of an author, T. Allen Winn. Problem with anything though, you can OD on it. The experience can consume you and take on a life of its own. I found it way too easy to talk about my writing, about my next book, the many projects, etc. Suddenly I went from pushing to pulling anyone who would listen to my tales of a newfound world. Blinded, I did not realize that everyone did not want to live and breathe my experience every waking moment. Jesus sent out the disciples in pairs to spread the word. He got it. He did not want to be the only one in the spotlight. Lesson learned, too much time in the spotlight is not good for you and it is not good for others. Obviously, I do not have twelve disciples at my beck and call to spread my accomplishments. The bigger picture here is not to be so self-centered, making people believe that you think you are the only one who can do what you do. It is not healthy for you and it is not healthy for those who believe in you. Now, I don't think Jesus was getting the big head. He just wanted others to spread the gospel, to take some of the attention off Him. It was not about Him. It was about God's word and the miracle of God.

That dream thing snagged me again. I do remember something that plays into to this scripture I read this morning. I dreamed that I was in an unfamiliar neighborhood looking for a mom and child I had previously met before. Some strangers greeted me and welcomed me openly. Others were suspicious of my roaming around there. Jesus sent the disciples in pairs to other neighborhood to spread the word. In the dream I was in another neighborhood seeking answers, trying to locate the mom and child. As I met others, we had conversations about this and that; some having nothing to do with my original purpose for being there. I don't think any of these were spiritual in content, but I was bonding with strangers, sharing my story while they shared theirs. In my mind, it is symbolic of the intent of the scripture. It is easier to move out of your comfort zone, into another neighborhood and speak openly and honestly while you are in search of something. Maybe in this dream it was preparing me for a larger purpose in life. One can make it be what you want. This is but my interpretation.

That brings me to the feeding of the five thousand, those five loaves and the two fish miracle. It does not seem possible that anyone could pull that off, stretching five loaves of bread and two fish to feed that many people. Why is it so easy to believe Jesus could cure the crippled, the leper, the comatose, others afflicted with all sorts of illnesses and then calm the waters to boot? If we believe those, why can't we comprehend that He can pull off the feeding of five thousand from meager rations? All that said, my takeaway as applicable is this. Never underestimate what you can do if you must. In life we need to be prepared to sometimes negotiate impossible odds. Spreading the word is not easy but it is not impossible either. It comes easier for some than others. For most of my life I have been an 'other'.

Right now, I remain in that other category and am not comfortable openly sharing my journey with others, so I journal it instead. That being confessed, I did share a bit with a close friend today at work. I explained to her how Sammy's death had impacted me and how I had taken that first step with Pastor Buddy. Now I did not spew the Holy Ghost or gospel in a way that I was pushing any repenting ways. I just laid it out, how I was early in the process and was still uncertain as to where it was taking me. This was another huge step for me in the process, me sharing this with anyone. I suppose spreading God's word on even the smallest of stage is a step in the right direction. Not a Bible totter yet, but as Pastor Buddy told me, I do not have to be. I am living and learning, incredibly early in the curve right now. That dream, just possibly this is where it gains merit. I found a need to share the beginning of my journey. No, it was not with a stranger, but it might as well have been. I had never talked this talk with anyone outside of Judy and Pastor Buddy. From my neighborhood to yours, Life is Good, God is Good. Keep on pulling.

Life's Recycle Program

Today's devotion, still in Mark, some of the scripture was quite familiar, even though I had not read it before now. As a kid, one of the memorable Sunday school lessons was always the one about Jesus walking on the water. It had that Sci-Fi, superhero appeal for those of us mesmerized by things almost too wild to imagine. The disciples got caught up in the wow factor too, terrified by what they were witnessing, thinking He was an apparition out there on the surface of the sea. Even the disciples had a tough time believing, but they hadn't quite gotten over that five loaves and two fish thing and the feeding five thousand. Weak moments and miracles can overwhelm the diehard followers.

I guess it also makes it easy for the non-believers, the naysayers, rationalizing that all the supernatural stuff that is documented in the Bible did not really happen. Was it a product of overactive imaginations or just myths and stretched truths? One thing for sure, Jesus was not shy about working them but then he would caution those that he had healed and those who had witnessed it to keep it to themselves. I am not quite getting this part yet, unless His intent all along was to tell them not to, knowing they would, and by them doing so, it was just another way for spreading God's word. Still, it seemed he was digging Himself a hole, one that eventually He would not be able to escape. One man's opinion in the early stages of the pull and no, I am not questioning His intentions nor the Bible nor God; I am just trying to digest and understand it.

Speaking of digestion, it ties in the next portion of my morning devotion. The Philistines and some religious scholars were following Jesus. Maybe they were there to disprove his powers or learn from them so they could steal his secrets and use them for nefarious reasons. Apparently, cleanliness was indeed close to godliness for them because they were taken aback when the disciples did not wash their hands before consuming their food. They even called Jesus out on, pointing out that it polluted the body, using unclean hands and touching the food like that. Jesus was quick to point out that it did not harm anyone, and He explained in detail the consumption of food and the purging of it from the body. He was more concerned about the harm, the pollution and the contamination did to the heart being impacted and not digesting a laundry list of items, lust, by adultery, etc. These things have a greater impact than the consumption of food with unwashed hands. Jesus was about keeping it real, sometimes in unrealistic ways.

I cannot help but pause for a second and mention how this is a controversial point between Judy and me. She uses that hand sanitizer and diligently washes her hands, almost too much in my humble opinion. I am at the opposite end of the spectrum. I joke saying I grew up playing in the dirt, outside most of the day and probably eating dirt as well. I never washed my hands back then until we had meals and was reminded that I was supposed to. As an adult I just do not get bent out of shape with the germophobic nonsense. I do not like those hand sanitizers because they burn my hands and dry them out. I wash my hands when I feel I should wash them, but that part of life just does not freak me out. Now, I am not saying 'that I told you so', that Jesus's big picture approach justifies me not washing my hands as often as she does, but it does put things in perspective as to what really matters when you get right down to it. I never thought about it in these terms until now.

I have certainly violated God's pollution guidelines over the years. I am sure I don't corner the market on this. I have allowed plenty pollutants to enter my heart and to disrupt life's digestive system. In my mind, I justify stuff by comparing myself to the real rule breakers, the worst of the worst, those that do not believe in God or are hypocritical in their beliefs, pot calling the kettle black in most cases. I guess that is why a part of me refuses to commit to certain things in the church. I have convinced myself that if I do so and am not whole heartily on board then that makes me a hypocrite by just going through the motions. Sure, I attend church, feeling it is my obligation to do so and often I am taken in by the lesson preached but I still push back on the essence of the full experience. It's almost as if I am protecting myself by not being someone that I'm not. If I don't pretend to get it, I'm somehow not held responsible to the greater cause. Jesus spelled it out for those that acted similar back then, those justifying their actions to fit their narratives. Today I guess you could make the analogy of fake news to fake faith. Not sure if I am making my case but this is just the way I have approached it.

I have made the internal argument that I am not a bad person. I believe in God. I go to church. I participate in some church activities. I never use the Lords name in vain. I do not talk in church when I am not supposed to talk. I certainly do not bring beverages into the church like so many do now. I abide by the rules and requirements when they fit what I think I am supposed to do. It is no wonder my spiritual digestive system is so out of sorts. I am diligently working on the cure, slowly but surely. I am seeing the light so to speak, and am working to understand it and fix it. Baby steps still but I am taking the steps one at a time. I'm sure I have plenty of falls in my future as I learn to walk within the light and navigate with unsure footing. The fact that I am reading, and rationalizing is a huge step. I continue to have my nightly prayer before bed. I am praying for others and not necessarily for me. I do need prayer but not in the way of asking for possessions or random favors, quick fixes and so forth. I get that part. It is not all about me. It is all about getting me right though.

You knew I was not going to wrap this up without bringing in that dream thing. I will keep it brief this time. I have no real recollection of any dreams from last night and it continues to be a bit troubling. My brain does not shut down normally at night. It remains active. I often struggle at bedtime because the button for shutting down my mind seldom works. It carries over into my dreams. I have this uncanny ability to almost force myself to wake up after I have had a vivid dream. I then replay it all night in my head so that I do not forget any of the details before I have an opportunity to document it. And yes, I drift off course and ramble as well. Scribblings in a journal, what can I say.

I am a detail orientated and driven person, almost compulsive at times. Not dreaming or not remembering dreams disturb me more than I can explain. Maybe it is a cleansing process. My dreams have just been an extension for my escape. Maybe I no longer need this tool, or I am being weaned off it to be replaced by what the pull holds in store. Enough, I will stop it here for now. I think this conversation is far from over though, at least for me. I must remember I am less than 9 days into this journey since that first meeting with Pastor Buddy. One thing for sure, it is easier for me to put my thoughts to print than through conversation. I am not ready to discuss this just yet. There is no right or wrong way to get there I keep reminding myself, Pastor Buddy's philosophy, not mine.

And by the way, you must have noticed by now that I do not list verse or scripture numbers. To me it is irrelevant in the big picture. It is like trying to remember chapter numbers. In my humble opinion and as it pertains specifically to me it serves no purpose. What is important is that I am taking time to have the devotions. I am taking my time reading them so that I can retain, understand, relate, and apply the teachings. And I am taking small bites of the apple as not to choke as I chew. *The Message* does make the reading much easier, putting into words and terms that I can understand, a blessing for us beginners. I highly recommend it, but everyone must tackle what best works for them. The main objective is not to approach this as a mere exercise and necessary evil. If you do, you may as well call it quits before you start.

You must feel that pull or some semblance of a need. If not for the circumstances, Sammy's death, its impact on me and the other related events, there is no way I would be where I am now. I would be aimlessly stumbling through life still, oblivious to the alternative. Force feeding this probably leads to failure. Listen to me. Suddenly I think I am an expert or something. I have a long way to go before I should consider tutoring or mentoring others. Like me, you must find your own way, your speed to travel the straight and narrow pathway. It does not matter how you arrive, right? You can arrive feet first, tucking and tumbling or sliding into first, just so long as you arrive.

Dream-Lame

Cutting to the chase, over the weekend I did dream but none of the dreams played had a bearing on my reading of the Word or the events of the weekend. Thusly I refer to these as lame dreams. I do slightly remember bits and pieces, but they are foggy at best. There I said it. Two days worth of lame dreams did not contribute to the lessons learned. Continuing in Mark because I am a slow reader and prefer taking time to let it take set, this would be a two-for reflecting time.

Jesus was a mighty busy man. As mentioned, I remembered the story of feeding those five thousand with next to nothing in loaves and fish, but I did not know it had happened again, this time with four thousand followers. The disciples were running a bit short on patience, guessing how they were going to feed this next horde. Seven loaves did the trick this time and they even had leftovers. Those benefiting from yet another miracle were in awe. The Pharisees were not so taken and physically threatened Jesus. He would not be bullied though, nor would he raise a hand to them. Jesus warned the disciples to keep an eye out for contaminating yeast of Pharisees and Herod's followers. He goes on to heal a blind man later.

He asks the disciples 'Who am I?' Peter speaks up and tells him He is Christ, the Messiah. Jesus then sets the scenario, how He would suffer, be killed, and after three days rise up alive. He points out to those who plan to go with Him that He must be accepted as the leader. He warns them that if any of them are embarrassed by Him when they are around friends then they will be shocked when He arrives in all the splendor of God, his Father, with an army of holy angels later.

Wow. What a powerful message for all of us, especially me.

Pastor Buddy's sermon ironically played into this scripture. He was reading from Luke instead of Mark. The choir sang Amazing Grace. This song was my mom's favorite and was played on the organ by our eleven-year-old grandson, Duncan Singleton at her funeral. He had never played the organ at Chandler-Jackson Funeral Home until then. And he played it because I asked him. Pastor Buddy gave me a book to read. I picked it up just before church began. A purple tie and bow marked the book on his desk where he told me it would be. The book was *The Men of the Bible* by James Stewart Bell. Boy how far I have come in such a short time. Still taking those baby steps though, keeping up with the pull as best I can. I am still feeling good from the inside out. I always joke that I smile on the inside. This time it holds true. The light is flickering, and the ember is burning brighter. I am hopefully getting there at my own speed.

Digression Indigestion

During that first meeting with Pastor Buddy Phillips, I openly shared with him how I had developed the push when it came to church. Judy had heard these stories before, and I had basically told her that I could not be forced to buy into all this Christian stuff because of the incidents that had shaped my resistance. After nearly twenty-three years of marriage, she had all but given up hope that my heart could ever be touched by God. Me too and here is why.

I grew up in a Pentecostal Holiness Church. Most of the relatives on my mom's side attended the little church in Abbeville, S.C. My mama had grown up in the very same church. Her mom, Granny Bowie was a devout Christian. Daddy's family leaned toward the Presbyterian faith, attending Long Cane on the opposite end of town. You would think that I should have had a solid foundation. Things are not as they might appear. As I have stated, Mama and Daddy did not attend church on a regular basis. I still think it was Mama sort of rebelling against having had to attend church regularly as a kid. Every Sunday though, before church dismissed, we would be at Granny and Papa Bowie's house preparing to have Sunday dinner with them. Granny would cook the meal on Saturday, not believing in cooking on the Sabbath. I know, you are asking what this has to do with my church phobia. It is a bit more complicated than just not regularly attending as a kid.

Let's fast forward to when I was a pre-teenager. I think I was attending church with Granny and Papa. Maybe I had spent the night with them after Papa and I had fished all day Saturday. During church, the preacher called the youth to come to the altar. Either Granny made me go or I followed the flock. I ended up there with the rest of the sheep. The adults gathered around us, placing their hands on our heads, prompting us to feel the touch of the Holy Ghost. Granny was all over me, talking crazy gibberish. She was speaking in tongues, something I had never experienced and did not understand. The ordeal continued, adults shouting and dancing about, prompting the youth to do the same, to give our hearts to the Lord. I must confess, it was quite terrifying and traumatic. That push thing did not set well with me and I pushed back, refusing to go where they wanted me to go. That was the last and only time I ever answered the call to the altar. I did not get it and I was not about to let it get me. It was just too scary.

I'm sure Granny Bowie was disappointed, but I was the poster boy for dishing out disappointment. My will and stubbornness are stronger than yours. Push me. I push back. The church scene was not doing it for me. Oh, I believed in God. That was not the problem. I was the problem. My heart was not open to this spiritual frenzy stuff. As a teenager with a driver's license, I began attending church Sunday nights but not in search of the Holy Ghost. It was a place to meet girls and to hang out with friends. I drew the line when it came to singing and praying though. I was a silent participant. I learned my craft at an early age. Soon though, even this ran its course, the push getting a bit too close. I got out while the getting was good. Girls could be found elsewhere. There were plenty of other places to gather with friends too.

The girl that I would eventually take as my first wife also attended this church. She and her family attended church regularly. As we began dating, I attended with her. The things you do for love, not necessarily for love of the church or the Lord. Others, including her, her family and my grandparents might have been buying it, but it was merely symbolic. I was a silent participant and there would be none of that altar stuff for me still. I am not trying to portray myself as this ultimate evil person. I just was not a joiner. Same went for school. I participated in no clubs, no sports, or cliques. I have often been pegged as loner. I guess the shoe fits. Might have something to do with that only child persona with a smidgen of stubbornness and the 'got to be me' complex.

Fast forward. Wedding planned. Daddy was set to be my best man. I was eighteen years old. She was seventeen. We had known each other all our lives but had not begun dating until our senior year in high school. The day of our wedding, Daddy and I waited in the preacher's office while folks arrived at the church. I can visualize this day like it was yesterday instead of January 22, 1972, which so happened to be Daddy's birthday. The preacher stepped inside, going over important stuff with us and then out of the blue he let into Daddy. He got in his face and began lecturing him about not attending church. This was my wedding day. It was Daddy's birthday to boot. Daddy, a man of few words, said extraordinarily little to the preacher's tongue lashing. I was furious. It felt like a set-up. This was not the time or place for this. I think I might have said a few things in protest. One thing for sure, I never cared for that preacher after that episode. He performed the ceremony, but I had no choice in that, not on such short notice. I was a kid. What was I going to do, postpone the wedding and then explain why to those in attendance?

After we married, I pacified my new wife for a while and attended church with her. My heart was not in it though, especially with my ill feelings toward the preacher. We even attended Sunday school where I was asked to lead prayer once and only once. I refused. I was not feeling it, that push back thing coming into play. Even back then I had that screwy perception about attending church. You are supposed to attend for all the right reasons. I was not and I could not play pretend. At a young age I felt that made me a hypocrite. I refused to be one of those content on being loyal on Sunday and then doing their thing when not there. And I was not living a life that qualified me to be a regular church goer. I knew the difference between right and wrong and it was wrong to pretend to be a Christian. The Holy Ghost had its work cut out. Pushing back was one of my strong suits. Do not try to make me be something I am not, not something that I am not yet ready to commit myself to. You will not come out on the winning end. My will is much stronger than yours. I assure you. That was then and this is now. So, where will now take me? To be determined.

To Be the Man You Must First Beat the Man

A bit of an exaggeration but the reading of this morning's devotion made me think of wrestler Rick Flair's mantra, 'to be the man, you must first beat the man.' Still in Mark, Jesus takes Peter, James, and John high up on a mountain. His appearance changes from inside out, his clothes shimmering and glistening. They see Elijah, along with Moses in deep conversation. There is talk of building three memorials for Jesus, Elijah, and Moses. Poof, Jesus is the only one with the disciples. As has become the theme, Jesus swears his three disciples to secrecy. The disciples are still confused about all this talk of rising from the dead.

Jesus later heals a deaf and mute boy possessed by a demon. The disciples had been unsuccessful in casting out the demon and question Jesus as to why they could not purge the demon from the boy. Jesus basically tells them it must be done by prayer. Being the man and believing whole heartily is the answer as I see it. The lesson today also teaches how you must be willing to forfeit your worldly possessions to earn your rightful place in the front of the line. Most cannot or are not willing to do that. I certainly have miles to travel to walk in the steps left by The Man. My heart is turning for sure, in the power of the pull but I have much yet to understand and grasp. Miles to walk.

Discussion turns to divorce. I am struggling with this one. I have been divorced twice, and it says if a man or woman divorces their significant other and takes up with another you have committed adultery. I am not sure where that puts me. Forgiveness is all I can ask at this point. The commandments were written leaving little wiggle room. Jesus gave his life for us so that we can be forgiven. The way I see it, to be the man, you must first beat the man you once were. I am taking on my former self, but it might be a best two out of three before I can raise my hand in triumph. I am early in my match yet, so much to learn and understand. I read slowly, take a deep breath, and then try to sponge it in. Life lessons await me at every turn, every fork in the road. I travel cautiously, all senses on high alert as I travel the pages of the scriptures, searching for a new me before all is said and done. God is Good.

Suite 101

Reading the scripture of Mark, it is filled with miraculous feats of Jesus healing this person and that. He does this by touch, sometimes using His own spittle in the eyes to heal blindness. The crippled walk, the mute speaks, and the seemingly dead rise. Some sneak touches to be healed instantly. Ironically, I am in pain, my lower back whacked out and I cannot even stand straight. What I would not give for one of those healing touches. I pray and I do believe but it is not my time I suppose. Maybe my pain is not significant when compared to those who really need and deserve healing. Perhaps I have not arrived at my final destination thus it is not my time to be healed of heart and body. One must have a back up plan until that time is here. My chiropractor offers a free visit on your birthday month. It is May and today is a good day to cash in on the freebie.

I was in luck and secured an early morning appointment. Appropriately so, I arrive at Suite 101, his office, the placard on the wall adjacent to the door clearly spelling out Suite 101. This holds a significant reference in my heart. As you might recall, Cuz, My Brother, Sammy Cannon, referred to the guest bedroom at our Myrtle Beach home as Suite 101. After his death we officially named it Suite 101 in his memory. We even have a desktop sign stating just this. I put my faith and fate in Doctor Shirley's hands. No, he is not God, but he is a Godly man. He is not shy about letting that be known. I respect that in him.

As in any visit, we chatted about this and that, even before he got down to business. He updated me on his house project, a home he was building himself. He then, for reasons only he knows, began telling me about his two teenage daughters and how they constantly bickered. In his words, they hated one another. I asked him how he had time to spend time with family, working and building the house. He confessed that it was a challenge, adding that he had spent two minutes with his daughters, disciplining them for recent actions. He told them he did not want them speaking to one another, about one another and did not expect them to borrow each other's possessions, period. Failure to comply would result in him taking their cell phones.

Doc shared how he was displeased with the youth of today. In his time and mine, at eighteen you were considered to be an adult. Now, kids grow up too fast, thinking they are already adults, cursing, smoking, and drinking way too early and too much. He said they think they have the rights of adults before they experience adulthood. He was also disturbed by vulgar music and the despicable influence it was having on kids. No wonder kids were so depressed and suicidal he added.

With all this gloom and doom, he finished his comments by quoting scripture from Luke and how it applied to the world today and his daughters. Let me be clear. His conversation was not in the form of rants. He did not raise his voice or change the tone of his voice. Everything was a mere matter of fact. He was sincerely troubled with the challenges and utilized God's word to help him deal with the situation. He has things in perspective. Lessons come in all shapes and sizes; often when you least expect them. In Suite 101 today I received a blessing and today will be a good day, even if my body is not healed of this discomfort. Doc prescribed rest, ice, and Advil. He also gave me reason to prescribe to God, inadvertently so.

I did as he had told me to do after he gave me an adjustment. I must confess, it was a painful day just the same. During my nightly prayer, only after I had prayed for others, I again slipped in one for me. Next morning, my bodily pain continued, no relief in sight. I worked on my spiritual pain, reading more from the scripture of Mark. Today's devotion introduced me to the question, what was the most important commandment? I had my guesses before I read on. Jesus answered, 'The Lord your God is one; so love the Lord God with all your passion and prayer and intelligence and energy.' And then he added a second, 'Love others as well as you love yourself. Why, that's better than all offerings and sacrifices put together.'

You must pick the pecking order. Putting yourself first is never going to fly. You must first love God and then love everyone else. Doc Shirley always ends our visits saying for his patients to have a blessed day. This lesson prepared me for my second visit to his Suite 101 in as many days. It also warned me as did Jesus to be aware of doomsday deceivers and how he told the disciples to be prepared to run for the hills when the final days arrived. No one knows the day or time when this will happen, nobody but God. I know it is not supposed to be my job to merely attempt interpreting what I read but it is by nature what we tend to do. I am no different.

There are spurts where I feel it and then there are other times where I do not. I cannot explain either. I am supposed to turn it over to Him. I get that part, but it's not as easily done as told. I don't know if I am trying too hard or not hard enough. Pastor Buddy said I was being pulled. Maybe I still have a little push left in me. My journey continues, trying to embrace the experience in heart and body. Be patient Lord, it took me nearly sixty-five years to get to this starting place. I am not giving up so please do not give up on me. My ailing back is on the road to recovery. Hopefully, my heart is heading down a similar path, my speed, no right or wrong way, keeping it between the lines and in the pull. Words are simple. Actions speak volumes. Wherever this is headed it has been amazing so far, an incredible journey.

Third consecutive day of Suite 101 visitation is in store for me today. That's later. Let me begin by sharing my devotion this morning and the uncanny associated events thereafter. Mark's word, Jesus was still preparing his disciples for what was to come, his death and how they would handle it. Again, I have heard these stories in sermons plenty of times, but I am just now reading them the first time via The Message. He tells them that a traitor is among them without naming him. He tells them they will deny knowing him three times once the traitor had perpetrated his betrayal. All comes true of course and the traitor is identified as Judas. How many times has that term been used, 'don't be a Judas or you are a Judas?'

The religious scholars and leaders do everything within their means to incriminate Jesus with crimes punishable by death. With a narrative they are determined to stick to, to conform to their premeditated agenda, they fabricate what is needed to justify crimes and a death sentence. And, the disciples, fearful of being caught up in this, deny knowing Jesus. The naysayer mob does not hold back on their mistreatment of this man who claims to be the Messiah. The script has been written and they stick to the script to spread their narrative. Sound familiar.

Devotion and reading of the scripture have this uncanny ability to bring it home and make it relevant in today's world. My typical morning goes, after showering and so forth, I have coffee while I catch up with the news. Mostly I watch Fox, but I will flip back and forth between CNN and MSNBC just to view their take on the morning's events. Seldom do CNN and MSMBC align with the events of the day or with Fox but they do stick to a common narrative. There mission is always to discredit the president and spread negative views aimed at formulating a selective narrative to destroy him. Never in my lifetime have I ever witnessed such disrespect for the presidency and the persistence to ignore any good accomplishments. Nor have I ever seen such a biased media no longer content with just merely reporting the news. It is sad to witness.

Let us zero in on a segment on MSMBC this morning. Morning Joe had a couple of guests, the discussion being the evangelistic spin they were putting on the support for the president. They were basically saying how so many evangelists and their flock were turning their backs on their faith and beliefs to support this despicable president. The network's spin, they were only doing it for four years to advance their narrative, the appointment of Supreme Court judges to support evangelistic needs. The segment focused on discrediting leaders of faith, pointing out several by name. Governor Mike Huckabee had been quoted as saying, 'We didn't elect a Minister in Chief' when he responded to those critical of the president's non-political approach. Sound familiar. It made me think.

Like back then, there are those trying their best to tear down and discredit any Christian faith. No God in schools, on judicial grounds, in the military, in the pledge of allegiance, holidays and, of all things, money. As the attacks were on Jesus, they continue today against Christianity. There is a Judas movement out there, intent on bringing it down, fake news in the worst way. From the pages of the scripture to the television screen, the similarity is a bit scary. Tough lessons are a hard pill to swallow. Our president has done everything within his power to recognize Christ in every possible way he can. That has irked those doing everything they can to snuff out His existence. When you want to remove Christ from Christmas when His name is part of the holiday and celebrating Him is the reason for the holiday, what is wrong with this picture? I am not attempting to make any sort of political statement. I am just applying common sense to a senseless situation.

Third visit to Suite 101 was the most effective according to Doc Shirley. Time will tell but I am a believer in his chiropractic miracles. Sounds crazy doesn't it. Me being a believer in something. He advised me to go to a medical doctor and get a prescription for muscle relaxer medication or buy a back brace to support my lumbar. I opted for a back brace. The journey continues, even with the old back out of whack. I am feeling my age, but I am a youngster in this process of following the pull and seeking God.

I did venture for my fourth day in a row to Doc Shirley, my only times leaving home this week. He felt we were making progress and then told me that I needed two things to assist my back in getting better. I told him I would bite and asked what. He said, 'Time and patience.' Two words, a profound message reaching beyond the confines of his office. Time and patience, heed to the pull, giving to time and patience, allowing the process to take shape, no right or wrong way, no timetable. As my heart continues its healing process I can only hope and pray that my ailing back follows suit.

Pre-Birthday Wishes and Blessings

I received the following from Judy Cannon, Cuz's wife, arriving the day before my birthday. No words from me are necessary. I scanned them and posted them below. Warning…keep a box of tissue within reach as you read.

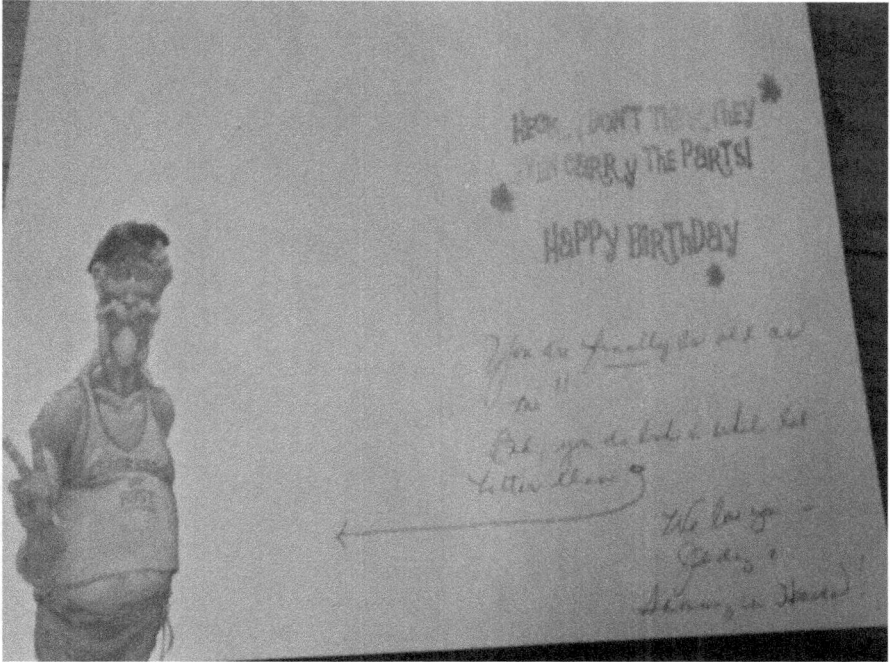

Tommy,

Judy shared with me the most
UNDERFUL news. It made me cry.
I know exactly what happened: Sammy
made a personal appointment with
Jesus. After Jesus listened to Sammy's
LONG story about his special cuz and
brother, the sighed and said, "Sammy,
I will handle this. You will see
your brother in Heaven one day".
   Praise the Lord!

Remember, no two people worship the
same nor pray the same. There are
even times I can't pray but Jesus
intervenes. Hold to your faith
My devotion the other morning made
me think of you so I've enclosed
a copy

   God bless you on this new journey.
                  I love you & Judy
                     SO MUCH —
                        Judy

82

Growing Up Without Giving Up

Rather, let our lives lovingly express truth [in all things, speaking truly, dealing truly, living truly]. Enfolded in love, let us grow up in every way and in all things into Him Who is the Head, [even] Christ (the Messiah, the Anointed One). — EPHESIANS 4:15

Growing up spiritually is not always easy. It might be said that we believers have to endure many "growing pains." Due to the challenging times, often we are tempted to give up. We all need to realize the progress we have made.

Perhaps you have been struggling with yourself. You know that you need to change. You desire to be like Jesus. And yet you feel that you are making no progress. The first thing you must realize is that you are making progress. Little by little, you are changing.

Take some time and think about where you were when you first accepted Christ into your heart. Listen to the Holy Spirit instead of listening to the devil! The way to listen to the Holy Spirit is by following your heart — not your head or your feelings. Learn to live beyond your feelings.

Don't compare yourself with other people. Everyone has strengths and weaknesses. Be patient with yourself. Keep pressing on and believe that you are changing every day.

Don't give up! You are growing up!

Say This:

"Christ is my life. I grow up into Him Who is the Head. Through Him I have joy unspeakable and full of glory!" (1 Peter 1:8 KJV.)

85

Re-Birth-Day

May 25, 2018, 65 years on this earth has officially arrived. Feeling it too with my old back still out of sorts and not how I had envisioned it. Winding up my devotion and journey through Mark, the morning scripture included the crucifixion and resurrection. I likened it to my rebirth too as my quest continues. Ironically, Judy gave me a birthday card this morning with her first written words saying. "How appropriate that May be your rebirth month, always to be remembered as the most important day in our married life."

Rebirth. Certainly not a concept I had ever envisioned. A lot has happened since losing Cuz. A hole in my heart for one has been a tough wound to heal. His death impacted me more than losing my parents and grandmother. I did not think anything could ever come close to that loss. It did though. Crazy how Sammy's death ironically led to my rebirth. It led me down a path I never stumbled upon before. Pain and sorrow are no more unique than losing a loved one, so how can one so powerfully impact a person's life for reasons never fathomed. Death leads to rebirth. What a concept!

Jesus gave his life for us to cleanse our sins. Sammy did not die to cleanse mine but in his death, I definitely stumbled blindly into purpose. What is life or death without purpose? Why do I suddenly think and rationalize in such profound terms? The television program *Touched by an Angel* comes to mind. No, not the premise of the plot but instead the power of the touch.

I read this list on a Facebook posting. Seems to be a reasonable course to follow if you really think about it. It was titled the 12 Steps for Self Care.

1) If it feels wrong do not do it
2) Say exactly what you mean
3) Do not be a people pleaser
4) Trust your instincts
5) Never speak badly about yourself
6) Never give up on your dreams

7) Do not be afraid to say NO
8) Do not be afraid to say YES
9) Be kind to yourself
10) Let go of what you cannot control
11) Stay away from drama and negativity
12) Love

I know what most must be thinking. Best advice, refrain from spending too much time on social media. Much of it is bias and manipulative if not just addictive. Normally I would blow past posts like this, but something pulled me to it. I am not categorically saying this was caused by God but with the current state of my being I was drawn to it. Maybe because of this rebirthing process for lack of a better explanation. Self care is part of the self awareness process. The evolution of the rebirth process does come with certain parameters. Maybe it isn't precisely what was posted but perusing these twelve steps does make a compelling argument.

1) If it feels wrong do not do it – *Understanding wrong and applying right is reasonable and the path best followed.*
2) Say exactly what you mean – *Now this one might get you in trouble. I can confess that too many times I speak before I think through the words that can be harmful or can be taken wrong. I interpret this more as meaning what you say and to not say them unless you mean them. Once out of your mouth you are stuck with consequences.*
3) Do not be a people pleaser – *Jesus did not say and do things because He wanted to be politically correct or to suck up to those intent on harming him. He spoke the truth and spread God's word and faced the consequences for doing so.*
4) Trust your instincts – *Your gut usually does not lie. If something feels wrong, it probably is. If on the other hand it feels right go with it.*
5) Never speak badly about yourself – *There is nothing worse than putting down yourself or lacking confidence. Look at me. I shied away from church related stuff. Refused to publicly pray or give grace. I often play the poor pitiful me card because I lack self esteem sometimes.*

6) Never give up on your dreams – *First you must have those dreams. Secondly, you must remain true to yourself and be who you are. In my case, becoming a believer and follower of the Lord did not come easily.*

7) Do not be afraid to say NO – *Peer pressure is the worst corrupter in my life. Trying to be the one you never dared at all cost instead of saying, are you crazy, I am not doing that.*

8) Do not be afraid to say YES – *Committing to Christ. Saying Yes when Yes counts the most. It was a tough lesson learned for sure.*

9) Be kind to yourself – *It was easy for me to put myself down in certain situations claiming I sucked at certain things or could not do certain things. Church and everything that goes with it was not something I was worthy of participating in whole heartily. Or so I convinced myself.*

10) Let go of what you cannot control – *Pretty simple but a tough lesson for me to grasp. Turn it over to God and it will work out as intended. No. It might not work out like I wish it to but once you sincerely put your faith in Him then the outcome is irrelevant to your own desires.*

11) Stay away from drama and negativity – *Wow. I have been on both sides of this fence. I must say that as I have become older and bit wiser, I do not appreciate drama in my life. I must confess though that I still struggle with being too negative in many incidents, one habit I do struggle to break free from. I pray that God helps me through this one. Part of my learning curve and transformation.*

12) Love – *Powerful four-letter word. Love of God, Love of family, Love of life. Love of country. Love thy self. Keeping the faith and trying my best to stay on the path. Stumbling and bumbling often but a work in progress.*

Rebirth. No one ever said it was supposed to be easy. I liken it to the path I once traveled. Am I there yet? Not by a long shot but does the journey really ever end?

Outside the Clique In

This morning I ventured into the word of Luke in *The Message*. In the intro the author prepares the readers for the writing of Luke. It seems that Luke fights for the outsiders, those not belonging to a group but looking to belong. Outside the clique, not with the in crowd, explains most of my life. As stated, I was never a joiner, more of a loner. I guess I lacked the confidence to be a member of any of the social cliques. I evolved into to the disrupter, the sarcastic entity, the kidder, the jokester, the daredevil, my way of fitting in by being outrageous, the ultimate rebel without a cause. I related quite quickly to the premise of Luke and his philosophy. It will be interesting seeing where Luke takes me.

In the first scripture an angel comes to an old man in a childless marriage and tells him his wife Elizabeth will soon be with child. He scoffs, telling the angel that they are too old to have children now. Odd, reading this as my mama was an only child. Her given name was Mary Elizabeth Bowie. I was not planned and ended up being her only child. Now an old man and having been married three times, I have never been a dad. The only child theme stops with me unless there is one heck of a miracle out there. Highly doubtful though. The elderly couple are told by God that this child will be named John. My Papa Bowie's name was John. I am not sure where I am going with these notable coincidences other than noting them. Elizabeth gave birth to me and had been completely shocked by the pregnancy. Elizabeth of the bible gave birth to John and John was the father of my mama, Elizabeth. Where I play into this scenario is to be determined. Obviously, I am not a biblical personality by any stretch but is it trying to spell out some purpose for me, sixty-five years later? To be determined if I decipher my latest babbling thoughts.

Judy and I had our morning coffee on the deck in the back, a cool and refreshing morning as we sat in our glider rockers. Judy laughed saying we certainly fit the part of old people rocking away. A dove fluttered and perched on the railing just a few feet from us. Judy is petrified of birds and that fluttering sound; she always has been. She took the appearance of the bird in stride this time. As we watched, I noticed that the dove would fly to the ground and walk about picking up this stick and that until it found the perfect one. It would then fly across the street and land on the outstretched limb of a live oak tree. It would walk to the end of the limb, a concealed leafy area and place it there and then return to meticulously search for another. It repeated this exercise countless times. The dove was obviously preparing a nest to lay its eggs.

There is that birth correlation again. I commented to Judy how wondrous it was that a bird could construct such a precise nest in a tree, one capable of holding eggs and one that would stay in place through wind and rain, and do this with no hands, just a beak. She said, 'Guess the birds look at us and wonder what we do with out hands.' A dove gives birth to the next generation of doves, outside any normal clique, doing what must be done to continue to live and contribute to life's cycle. God is Good.

Sunday and Memorial Day

Sunday and today I simply give thanks for the Sabbath and for those who gave their lives so that we could live free and worship as we see fit. I read more scripture from Luke. Jesus continued to wow his followers and make enemies of those who hated Him and what he stood for. Let us just leave it at that today and embrace what has been given to us by the blood of others, soldiers, and the Son of God.

'Every valley shall be filled in, every mountain and hill made low. The crooked roads shall become straight, the rough ways smooth.'

Déjà Vu

As I read the scripture of Luke, I feel I am in rewind mode, traveling down paths I have already traveled. Is it me or am I imagining it? I am seeing the same stories retold, those of healing the Leper, the cripple, etc. The birth of Jesus is told through Luke's perception maybe. I guess my question is the intent to share another disciple's perspective of the same events. I am not saying that I don't need to read things more than once for it to sink in or touch me as it is supposed to, but I am experiencing some redundancy in the first verses of Luke. If this supposed to teach me that people have different perspectives, their own spins. Time and patience, I remind myself as tossed out to me by Doctor Shirley. Again, I am not questioning the Bible, but as a detail-oriented person I can't help but notice stuff like this.

Yes, time and patience indeed. I will sit back, sponge it in and see if what I read this morning plays out into my today's activities. More times than not there have been undeniable signs, correlations to my morning devotions. It is to be determined if today plays out in similar fashion. I have received one blessing though. My aching back feels better than it has in the past seven days, one burden lifted hopefully. When I do my nightly prayers, I try not to focus on me but to focus on others that I am aware of that have medical challenges, emotion challenges or are experiencing tragic circumstances in their lives. I always pray for our president, our country, and the world. I must confess though. Selfishly, I have slipped in an occasional one for me over the last couple of days if He sees fit to cure my back while He still works on my heart.

How appropriate, I saw this post on Facebook this morning. It read…

One Sunday Morning at a small southern church the new pastor called on one of the elder deacons to lead the opening prayer. The deacon stood, bowed his head, and said, 'Lord, I hate buttermilk.'

The pastor opened one eye and wondered where this was going. The deacon continued, 'Lord, I hate lard.' Now the pastor was totally perplexed. The deacon continued, 'I ain't too crazy about plain flour. But after you mix 'em all together and bake 'em in a hot oven, I just love biscuits. Lord, help us to realize when life gets hard, when things come up that we do not like, whenever we do not understand what You are doing, that we need to wait and see what You are making. After You get through mixing and baking, it will probably even be something better than biscuits. Amen.'

Unlike the deacon, I love buttermilk and all the ingredients that contribute to a pan of cathead biscuits. Lord, toss in a bowl of homemade brown gravy and I think we are set. It does make you think though. Just remain patient and in due time God will work out what is most important and nourishing to be spiritually satisfied and full. Luke framing what he saw was just that. As a reader of the gospel, it is not for us to question the scripture as written even it is seen from another's eyes. Miracles are worth repeating and, in the end, they are still all inspiring and wonderous.

Wit-ful Thinking

Because this is another work week for me, my AM devotion has been disrupted somewhat. I must optimize a much more abbreviated reading technique. Luke did teach me a valuable lesson, one that even resonated through the speakers of my radio on my workday commute, but I will get to that in a second. Let us start first with the scripture of Luke and no, I will not be spewing actual verse, but only my interpretation, which The Message already does very well.

This one hit home quickly, bulls eye right between the eyes. Jesus basically instructed the disciples not to pick on people, attack their weaknesses, put them down or belittle them. I have mentioned previously I am quite proficient in sarcastic wit, always zooming in on a person's ill-fated and most uncomfortable mistakes, via their actions or something they might have misspoken. As I have been reminded, I have the memory of an elephant and I will file these occurrences away and strategically bring them back up years to come. Rubbing peoples noses in stuff that they did or said has become a trait that defines who I am. Those who know me, expect it from me. They might not like it, but it is expected. Those who do not know me do not always know how to take me. I have been told countless times that what I said was mean spirited when in my mind it was just kidding, all in good fun. I have always defended my wit and sarcasm by saying I only pick on those I love. The more I pick on you, the more I must love you. Those on the receiving end do not necessarily share my explanation.

Be kind to others, love thy enemies, and give more than you take. Boy, do I have an extreme transformation makeover in store if I am going to be who I am supposed to be. This is where time and patience play in big time for me and for those that I so love to pick on. I sure hope God will stick with me until I can see this through to the finish line. I always react to situations and circumstances, kicking into spontaneous wit and sarcasm. That has been my 'MO'. I even have a couple of tee shirts that profess this claim. I guess first things first, I should get rid of them if I am going to follow the pull. Controlling my tongue will be a huge challenge though. Time and patience will be tested.

As I commuted to work this morning, I had my radio tuned to talk radio. They began doing a segment about things that make you mad. Each of the co-host swapped incidents from the news and so forth. Liz Callaway mentioned one that particularly bugged her, television evangelist that tend to do what they can to ask for money more so than really walking the walk. In a recent news item, a television evangelist made the comment that if Jesus were alive on earth today, he would not be riding a donkey. He would be traveling by jet. Furthering his narrative, he then mentioned that he was asking for donations to purchase a 54-million-dollar jet for himself. He already owned three. Liz then attempts to quote scripture, unsure where it was specifically written, but basically saying that it was not so much about a person speaking the word, the gospel and attempting to make believers out of the rest of us, but living the life and people seeing you for who you really were, leading by example and not tooting your own horn. If you are a good person, people will see you for who you are. The pull has unique techniques to get its point across; first through the scripture of Luke and nailing me, and then thirty minutes later through the airwaves, a talk show host basically saying the same thing. I can almost see Cuz up there, elbowing God and saying, 'See, I told you so.'

Perspectives

I am still reading the book of Luke and continue to be somewhat confused because of the repetition. Luke tends to repeat what Mark had already shared, possibly in some cases from a new perspective but still the same Jesus scenarios. I am really trying to keep an open mind and learn from a second review so to speak but it is difficult when you realize you have basically just read this. I find myself too easily caught up in skimming through it rather than reading it word for word. I know I shouldn't be taking shortcuts by doing this, but bad habits prevail. I keep telling myself, I am new at this, time, and patience, no right or wrong way but is this really the appropriate approach? Uncanny, when looking for answers you receive one. I just read this on Facebook as posted by Walter Monroe who happens to be a cousin and a minister.

'Often when we are caught in the storms of life and overwhelmed by clouds of despair, we can easily fear that God has lost control of things and that we are at the mercy of fate. Not so! God is sovereign and we must remind ourselves of the question He asked His disciples: "Where is your faith?"

Despair might be an overstatement in this case, but the verse is applicable to my somewhat questioning ways. I must learn to practice and live faith. Perhaps Luke continued to toss in his perspective of incidents to help us (me) better grasp the significance of the Word and the miracles performed by Jesus. People tended to view situations, circumstances, or events differently. We apply our own slanted views. The disciples, as followers of Jesus, witnessed the many miracles He performed and sometimes perspectives differed. This is common and there is nothing wrong with it. What is important is that you grasp the big picture, right? Even a hard head like me can get that. Thank you, Cousin Walter, for the inspirational post.

Pocket Full of Change

I am pausing from reading The Message and began reading Men of the Bible. Something has drawn me from one to the other, the pull I suspect. Pastor Buddy gave me this book for a reason, even after he gave me those initial suggestions for reading Mark, Luke, etc. The author states that the reader should read one devotion each day. Supposedly the premise is to begin January 1st, each devotion dated thereafter. I started my January 1st one June 6th; one day at time, no wrong way so said Pastor Buddy. I am not saying The Message was not working for me, but I just felt compelled to try a different approach. But before I get too deep into my new book, something is not right.

The back issues persist but after nearly two months the pain has subsided enough to be tolerable. Newer, more concerning issues have developed though. But to explain, I must digress just a tad. Through those many weeks of almost nonstop back pain, I took over the counter pain medicine day and night. I wore the back brace much of this time and even used those hot-cold patches that sometimes offer temporary relief. Most nights the pain did not plague me in bed but the time my feet hit the floor that was a much different story.

It was marginally improving when I strained it again moving an outdoor glider rocker. This by far had to be the worst battle I have ever had with back problems. I feared I would become one of those elderly figures I have often seen stooped over and walking with a cane or walker. Doctor Shirley promised me that was not going to be the case. After a while, the second round of pain eased up again, enough to be manageable. During those weeks of back pain, I had difficultly with bowel movements. Sorry for the personal graphics but I have a point to make. That was a new one for me because I am an irregularly regular guy, two to three times daily. I chalked it up to the pain in the strain. After my back improved though, the constipation persisted. I became concerned with my precarious situation. So, what do you do when you have concerns and questions? You gravitate to the internet and begin researching symptoms. What did we do before the Net? We probably lived more sane lives.

Because my mom died of pancreatic cancer and experienced back pain, I first perused those symptoms. There were some similarities, but I researched further, next looking up prostate cancer. Again, there were some similarities. Then I Googled colon cancer and found scary similarities. I kept these concerns to myself for about a week. I turned to prayer, asking God to continue his spiritual healing of me and asked for physical healing. These are my prayers but remember, I am new at this. I have rarely included those for me other than the continuance of guiding me into the pull and faith in Him. Much of the scripture I have read has told stories of how Jesus cured people of many illnesses. Is it wrong to ask for these healing powers from God so early in my journey? I am not sure, but I am afraid, no denying that fact.

The words I have read so far tell me to put my faith in Him, my complete faith. I am struggling but I am doing my best to do just that. I finally told Judy my concerns. She shared my concerns with Judy Cannon and Rhonda Singleton, both adding me to their prayer list. Not that I have no faith in God, but practically speaking I felt the need to find a doctor and obtain a doctor's appointment. If my worst fear was true, the self diagnosis, then time could be a factor. I had recently lost my doctor of twelve years after turning sixty-five. She does not accept Medicare. I knew that months ago but had no real sense of urgency to seek a new doctor ahead of time. She had recommended a doctor, so I gave him a call. He was not accepting new patients. Every doctor I contacted was either not accepting new patients or appointments were one to two months out.

Concerned, I go to Doctor's Care, who my wife uses. They were just ten minutes away. I did not get to see a doctor, only a practitioner. I shared my concerns with her and all I got out of the visit was a recommendation to buy some Milk of Magnesia and evacuate my bowels. This did nothing to quench my concerns. I did what she had recommended, and it did what it was supposed to do. My bowel movements did not return to normal, but I was at least having them again. Other signs from the colon cancer list persisted. I tried to stay upbeat and continued my prayers, but they were there every day. I eventually secured two doctor appointments, the earliest still a month away and the second two months away. Again, time felt to be a factor but what do you do short of going to an emergency room. It felt urgent but was it an actual emergency?

The issues continue, the pull continues, and I put my faith in His hands.

Viral Inspiration

After reading this morning's devotion, I perused Facebook briefly before preparing for my first workday of the week, actually for the month since I only work one week a month in post-retirement life. I have handed my health concerns over to God but as strong as I try to stay the course and put my faith in His hands, I cannot help but be concerned. I guess I still struggle a bit putting the reigns in His hands. I am still two weeks away from my doctor's appointment. All that being babbled, who would have thought that my prayers might come in the form of a viral video on Facebook of all places?

In the video a young gentleman was boasting about the power of faith, of prayer and believing in miracles. He held firm to all and offered proof, evidence that God is real and that He listens to prayers and yes, can produce miracles when it is His will to do so. The young man had a friend whose mother had been diagnosed with a cancerous tumor in her colon. Like anyone would, she was very worried about her path going forward and what the doctors might or might not be able to do. The young man had his friend set up a video chat with his mother and him. He prayed for God to heal her. During this video prayer warrior session, the woman felt her belly get hot and experienced relief, both physically and spiritually. On her follow up visit to her doctor, to his and her surprise the MRI showed no signs of the tumor or cancer. Now that is what I needed to boost my day and reinforce my faith. I confided in my friend Carl, who has dealt with cancer battles over the years and even recently its ugly head has popped up with a friend of his. Carl's friend Joe battled cancer while Sammy did. Both Joe and Sammy lost their battles with the deadly foe. Carl and I have become remarkably close and can talk about anything. We ended our little powwow with a hug.

In Men of the Bible Peter Acts 12:7 jumped out at me and the theme, 'It isn't over until God says it's over.' Whatever you are facing, He will not abandon you. He will enable you to complete whatever He has planned for you. Powerful! I guess the million-dollar question is what does He have in his plan for me. I put my faith in Him. The pull keeps me on the righteous path. I continue to pray for my very own spiritual and physical healing.

My day at work today has been a better day than some recently. The abdominal discomfort has been at a minimum. I am not healed as I would hope to be, but I hold firm to the faith and His plan for me. In my heart, my obtaining a relationship with God at my age speaks volumes that there is more ahead for me and ways I can serve and spread the word with my newfound experience. No, I am a far cry from disciple material, but He chooses those that He thinks can serve and get the most bang for the bucks so to speak. I continue to be new at this and still am amazed at how I see things differently for the very first time. I have a new attitude and a new outlook. Yes, I do have my concerns, but it is only human to feel as humans do. Still, my faith grows stronger and I will allow it free reigns to take me where I need to go.

Revenge is Costly

Today's reading from Men of the Bible had to do with Joab (Samuel 3.27). I guess I have never been a revengeful person in the truest sense, and I have never seriously considered killing anyone but that does not mean I am innocent of all charges. It is easy to say or think 'I wish this or that person was dead' or 'I hope he or she get what they deserve.' When people anger you and betray you, you tend to think ill-willed thoughts toward them. When people tell me that they are going to do something, I expect them to be true to their word. Maybe people have good intentions in some cases and later find it difficult to follow through with their commitment. Fine, just be honest about it. Own it. Tell me that it is not going to work out before I discover you have betrayed your word. Cover ups only lead to regrettable circumstances. Harsh words exchanged. Deciding that you no longer have any use for a person and/or have spitefully abandoned the relationship, cutting that person out of your life. Sure. I have been down this path more times than I care to count. I have been on both sides of this fence. Neither are pleasurable experiences. It is not always easy to forgive or so I have experienced.

Making a point and speaking words you cannot take back eventually hurt you as much as the person on the receiving end. Reconciling a situation like this can be even more painful. No one likes to admit that they were wrong or be the first to say they are sorry. Eating crow is just that, no matter if you started the altercation or punctuated it to advance your agenda. Petty is petty and in the big scheme of things most of these disagreements or hurtful situations are just that. Wishing death on someone or hoping their world collapses gains you nothing if you really put a little thought into what you are asking. Still, we do it. We cannot seem to help ourselves. If we are not happy, we begrudge the person that caused us unhappiness too. Getting even is not really an even prospect. In God's eye it is simple betrayal on all counts.

Taking advantage of one's status, being the boss or a leader over someone does not anoint you with unlimited powers. You are not thusly empowered to use that authority to inflict physical or emotional pain on those of lesser authority just to prove your point or that you can do whatever you want to do. We were all made by the same Creator. Abusing your fellow man or woman is not going to fly in His eyes. It might not be on the level of committing murder, but it still holds the same consequences. Belligerent actions are tough to justify from His perspective. I am no expert on this stuff. I am in the infancy of the pull, but I am now trudging forth with my eyes a bit wider open. Am I there yet? Not hardly but I am learning and hopefully living a better life because of my new relationship with the Man up above.

I will close with one example where my worst practices have come into play. I have mentioned Carl a few times. Talk about an on again and off again personal relationship, we have covered both ends of the spectrum. Keep in mind that my account is a one-sided version. I can only share my feelings and will not try to decipher his thoughts or maybe his justified actions in how he perceived the situations. Most of our little fallouts revolved around the game of golf. Yes. A supposedly gentleman's game had ended in anything but gentlemanly results. And no, wagering played no part of the misunderstandings. I am aware of my limitations when it comes to life on the links. I never gamble on my ability to score well. Always attempt to bet on a sure thing. I am the furthest from that outcome. No odds are too great to make me a sure thing.

My friend tends to over promise and under commit when it comes to golf. Allow me to explain. He is our tee time scheduler for the same foursome for the most part, all work buddies from the company that I retired from in 2015. On a couple of occasions, he has either secured us a tee time or had agreed to play on a specific course and day. Twice that I can remember, he backed out of his commitment saying he could not play, only to find out that he played with another group. I felt that this infringed on our friendship. How can you treat real friends with such disrespect? I confronted him and went ballistic. How can you do this I protested.

Afterwards I avoided any social contact with him, cordially treated him as best I could as a coworker when the job required us to interact. I was miserable during these periods, ever so spiteful and angry with him. I am not sure how he felt or perceived our situation. I never asked. These usually continued for months or even longer, us not playing golf together. In most cases I do not recall how these were ever reconciled. I know that there were no spoken apologies from either side. I think when I found out he was battling cancer a second time a few years ago, I dropped by to wish him the best in the aggressive treatment he was undertaking. I think his situation trumped our petty differences. Sometimes things work out for a reason. I never thought about them in Godly or biblical terms. I just figured they just happened.

Let us fast forward to recent years. When Sammy was diagnosed with leukemia and especially after the real battle began for survival in late 2017, Carl became my confidant. He had fought cancer at least twice and was a survivor. He knew Sammy well and often played golf with Sammy and me when Cuz came to the beach. A relationship developed between Carl and me, something special, something probably neither one of us fathomed possible. During Sammy's battle, Carl had a friend up north also waging a battle with cancer. We would share updates on Joe and Sammy, always ending those visits with a manly hug. Carl has never been one to openly share that kind of relationship and I had never previously shared a hug with him. I think being a cancer survivor changed him. He had a new respect for life and a better understanding and appreciation for true friendships. We are indeed the best of friends now.

Sammy and Joe died days apart. Carl and I shared those awful moments of loss and grief. Two unlikely people have become best friends, brothers so to speak. Forgiveness is a powerful tool. Treating those as you would like to be treated speaks volumes. Hatred and vengeful thinking and actions are so wasteful in life on this earth. Living a life with your fate in God's hands lifts the heaviest of burdens. I would know. I am living and learning every single day. I have hurt too many people in a life not understanding His love and power. God is Good!

I saw the following posts on Facebook, and they all struck home…

I am a Christian

When I say that "I am a Christian," I am not shouting that "I am clean living." I'm whispering "I was lost, but now I'm found and forgiven."

When I say "I am a Christian," I don't speak of this with pride. I'm confessing that I stumble and need Christ to be my guide.

When I say "I am a Christian," I'm not trying to be strong. I'm professing that I'm weak and need His strength to carry on.

When I say "I am a Christian," I'm not bragging of success. I'm admitting I have failed and need God to clean my mess.

When I say "I am a Christian," I'm not claiming to be perfect. My flaws are far too visible, but God believes I am worth it.

When I say "I am a Christian," I still feel the sting of pain. I have my share of heartaches, so I call upon His name.

When I say "I am a Christian," I'm not holier than thou. I'm just a simple sinner who received God's good grace, somehow!

God can make
THE REST OF YOUR LIFE
BE THE BEST OF YOUR LIFE.
TRUST HIM.
HE HAS A PLAN FOR YOU.

Tony Evans

TONYEVANS.ORG

Whenever you do not understand what's happening in our life, just close your eyes, take a deep breath and say... "God, I know it is your plan. Just help me through it. Amen"

"lovely"

Follow Instructions

My devotion from Men of the Bible this morning had to do with Noah and the ark from Genesis 6:22, but as always, it provided a modern-day lesson for us newbies to relate to and understand. The example given was about a man who had bought a credenza that required full assembly. He did as he always did. He removed all the items from the pre-packaged containers and then began looking for the instructions. Good man right, not like most, meticulous enough to utilize the instructions. Unlike me, I tend to wing assembly jobs and if I have any parts let over, I dub them as extras. That is unless something is not working like it is supposed to be and I then discover the parts should have been added in one of the earlier steps. To be candidly honest, I despise assembling anything, but disassembling is not fun either.

Back to the story at hand. The man after being unable to locate the instructions noticed a warning on one of the boxes, boldly printed I might add. It basically warned that all boxes should be opened one at a time because items required in each step of the assembly were prepacked in that manner. Now the poor guy had everything sprawled about in front of him making a forty-five-minute job become a four-hour job. His best intentions had been derailed by not following the instructions as clearly marked on each box. The larger point from the author, always follow God's instructions and you will be rewarded. Noah did just that when preparing his family for the floods and building the ark precisely as instructed by God.

Lesson taught, so how do I apply this wisdom to my humble life? Where has God provided me with instructions to follow? I have always had this ability to color outside the lines when needed to complete the task at hand. I have justified this by proclaiming it is a gift to process the wisdom to be flexible and adapt. God sees things differently apparently if He is the one providing instructions and guidance. To coin my sister-in-law Norma's wording, 'He is the Head Nacho.' Yeah. She is notorious for word gaffs, but you must love her just the same. She is our Norm Crosby.

Me, remaining in the pull, is certainly His idea as pointed out by Pastor Buddy. But I believe there are more important matters at hand for me. Utilizing my writing skills to spread the word could be in play. I have already completed my (our) tribute to Cousin Sammy Cannon, 'Cuz, My Brother, Life is Good, God is Good' and in it I credited Sammy and a series of events after his death with opening my heart up to a relationship with God. Logging this journal is another important step in this journey. It is my belief that God instructed me to document the transformation for me firstly and possibly to help others see 'The Light.' I became a slacker for a few weeks and got away from it, allowing other matters to disrupt it, including worrying about my health issues. After watching that video, a couple of days ago and again turning the reins back over to God, ironically, this week while at work, I got back to it, writing my daily experiences and for the past three days I have felt physically better than I have in the last couple of months. My abdominal pain has been almost nonexistent, and I have found regularity in my bowel movements. Might it be His plan is for me to do this? Could I have been led to help others?

I have a friend that is quite liberal. I call him a liberal, atheist, vegetarian. Little Goober Head and I try not to talk politics because we are at extreme ends of the political spectrum. Sammy is the one who named him this during a golf outing and during one of their many golf wagers. Little Goober Head and I do not really talk food because I eat normal stuff and he eats mostly salads and fish. He does not believe in eating what he refers to as caged animals (cows, chickens, pigs, etc.) We never talked religion even though my beliefs were far different than his. I just never felt comfortable talking religion with anyone. Not that I was not a believer in God. I just never felt compelled or qualified to speak about it. The pull is changing that. My friend recently became a parent for the first time. He had wanted a child for quite a while and he and his wife had even tried egg implants, both ending in miscarriages. When they were contemplating one last expensive attempt his wife conceived. I do not believe I have ever seen him happier or prouder.

We exchanged these emails a few months after the birth of his child and after the death of Sammy. The first was from me to him, the second was his response to me.

I know your life has changed and has been blessed with the birth of your daughter. Given what you and she endured, I would say this is indeed a miracle. I know you do not necessarily believe in God, but I think He might have helped you in this one. Just as the birth of your daughter impacted your life, the death of Sammy altered the course of mine. I loved him like I have never loved another man. I miss him every day.

I just wanted to let you know that the 'Cuz, My Brother' book has been published and I will be placing an order for those who want a copy of the keepsake today. Because of the photos, some in color, this is a nonprofit book, just being sold at cost. Let me know if you would like one.

He replied,

First, of course I want a copy of the book. I would have liked Sammy to be my father-in-law had things worked out differently. I know what a loss it is for you.

Regarding my daughter, I do wish Sammy could have met her. I knew having a child would be a gift, but I did not know the impact she would have on me. I cannot explain how much I love her.

Maybe there is a higher purpose involved. I am open to that possibility. It gives me some comfort to think that Sammy is watching down on us now.

His response was a total shock, that part about believing a higher purpose might have been involved. First, it was so unlike me, 'the old me', to have ever articulated in terms of God. Then, he seemed touched by this, even saying it gave him comfort to think Sammy might be watching down on them. You cannot imagine what a breakthrough that is for him and for me. I am confident that I have been following instructions. I have been instructed to share my newfound beliefs with those who might need it as much as me. With my pal, Little Goober Head, it was an unexpected joy though. If I weren't so old and with bad knees, I would cut a few cartwheels about now. The pull is so powerful it has snagged even my friend in its wake. God is Good.

Defining the Faith at Home

Devotion of the day from Jude I:3 from Men of the Bible: premise of this one was to look around your home and identify the enemy to basically protect your family. Before I review this though, first I must share a post that I saw from Judy 2, Cuz's bride, before I began my reading. It was the perfect start for an inspirational day.

From Judy,

As we grow older, I believe we become more immune to the struggles in life or at least I have. I am one who loves even when someone becomes "unlovable". I forgive easily and I don't hold a grudge. I quickly forget why I got upset with you in the first place. Maybe you call it early stages of dementia! I call it LIFE. I was not placed on this earth to judge or to cause pain to anyone else just because I feel the need to "get back at them" or "prove a point". I am NO saint- far from it - but I do know that life is short, but life is good. Losing Sammy has made me even more aware that we don't always have tomorrow so live each day doing what glorifies Him, yet I often fall short. We may not understand why things happen to us, why it seems our world is dishing out bad things, but we don't have to know why. We just need to trust and know He will take matters into His hands. "vengeance is mine, says the Lord". It isn't ours. I rest in that when I want to take matters into my own hands. I don't have to. As Sammy said so much in his last months of life, "Life is good and God is good" or "We will take it one day at a time". It's such a peaceful feeling to know that no matter what we are taking care of, if we just put our troubles, our fears, our anxieties in God's hands it will all come out for the good.
I'm really not sure why I wrote this tonight at 12 AM other than I feel at peace with certain situations because I believe!!! I am just off on one of my spiritual rampages and I like it!!!

Well said Judy 2. Now back to the devotion as mentioned. Devotion of the day from Jude I:3 from Men of the Bible: premise of this one was to look around your home and identify the enemy to basically protect your family. Family defined for us is just Judy and me. I can see where this can require much more thought when children are involved. The enemy could take on the form of the television with specific harmful programming. Unwanted influence on children can obviously be the result of video games. I am an old Atari game player if that tells you anything. I am talking the original Atari. Graphics were cool but back then we had stuff like Pong, Frogger, Pacman, Missile Invaders, Smurfs, but nothing with graphic violence like there is today. I say that but I have never played video games beyond those Atari days and can only go by what I have heard others describe or what I have seen on commercials about the newest kill fest available for family entertainment. Murder and mayhem are taught through these games so say the critics.

Public enemy #1, most of us are caught up in the social media world to some degree. We have smart phones, laptops, tablets, Kindles, etc. Do any of us use these in moderation or with any common sense? Toss in Snapchat, Twitter, Facebook, and many of the other venues I have no clue how to navigate or desire to learn, and you have the perfect recipe for unruliness and hateful behavior. Plus, the generation of today is quickly losing the ability to communicate, relying too much on text, chats, Instagram, sometimes when they are just feet apart. I do not have kids but if I did, I would never allow mine to have a cell phone until they were old enough to understand the ramifications of abusing it and disrespecting their parents in the use. It irks me when I see children that must be seven-ten years old with cell phones or other electronic devices always in their possession, their faces buried downward. Children and adults alike must be developing bad posture with the constant use and positioning of their craned necks. And what about the corrupting of their minds and souls, it is not a pretty picture.

I am guilty of using these devices. I have a Smart phone, a Kindle and two laptops. I use and read Facebook. I text. I email. That is about as far as I go. Have I posted Facebook stuff that I should not have? I have but I have also learned from those stupid consequences. I primarily use it now to promote my books or chat with family and friends. And, I try to skim pass the garbage, the vile and hateful postings. As anything, you must exercise discipline and restraint. As a parent your responsibilities should include teaching your children how you expect them to use them and if they abuse that privilege then they lose the use of them. I know, easier said than done coming from a non-parent.

From an outsider looking in, in my humble opinion, the parents can be tossed onto the enemy list. Poor parenting breeds all the above. It creates the environment for the ugliness, lack of discipline, attitudes, and perceived entitlements so many kids expect. It starts in the home and the faith inspired by those who rule the roost and stand as role models for those they brought into this world. YOU cannot ignore that responsibility or pass it on to someone else, like teachers. YOU owe it. YOU are the mentor. YOU are the one who delivers the discipline if these guidelines are not met. Tough love is just that, but it works. Set an example, how about it? Teach them to respect themselves and to respect others; enough said.

So, what is my takeaway from this morning's devotion and how it specifically impacts the Winn home, two adults, no kids within the household? Who are our enemies? Obviously, all the devices I have already mentioned, if not utilized wisely. At this point in our lives, I certainly feel like we have the discipline to make the best choices to properly defend the household, that being us. The enemy can also be us. Out of the mouth can often come hurtful thoughts, and even worse, allowing what has occurred as a result, to fester. Apologize, talk it out as quickly as possible because life is too short as it is to live it miserably. Better still, practice restraint. Keep that foot out of your mouth. I suffer too often from foot in mouth disease. If you do not say harmful things, then those things cannot harm you and your relationship. Again, I struggle with this speak before you think issue. My mind races too quickly and I often butt in and speak over people. Not intentionally but it happens. It is almost as if my thoughts are so intent on escaping my brain at all cost they leap from my mouth as if I am the only one important in the conversation.

This has been one of my most difficult things to control. I too often say something I did not really mean to or I say something that is taken the way I did not really mean it to be taken. Sometimes it is in the delivery. I have a loud and sometimes excitable voice. Often, I sound mad or belligerent when I am not. I have the reputation of being extremely sarcastic and love to pick at people, especially when I have something on you. I have tried to curb these temptations. Am I there yet? No, but I am trying to do better. Being considerate of others, putting them first before myself, are things I am still working on. Selfish habits are hard to break but not impossible. The 'ME' first factor cannot exist or the enemy wins, hands down.

I am learning that the best way to defend the home and defeat the enemy is to have faith in Him. Turning over my faith and trust in Him will crush any enemy invasion. Sure, I may lose a battle here and there but ultimately the spoils go to the winner of the war. God is Good, and if you believe in Him and put your faith in Him and live by Him, no enemy can defeat you. Defending your home is a way of the past. An unwanted invader cannot breach the doorway or your heart. I am getting there at my speed, in my way. Proof is in me reading my daily devotion, learning from what I read and applying it and writing this journal. They all play a part in the bigger picture. I desire to be part of that bigger picture and rely on God's plan to get me there.

Writer's Privilege

My life, my journal my way…so, I am changing gears from the theme, the pull I have been following. Reading devotions and interpreting them has served a valuable purpose in my evolution process. But wait, as those info-commercials go for those got to have gadgets, there is more. Due to a combination of reasons, I had drifted away from journaling for quite some time. The fact that I had should not be interpreted as a sign that I have been back sliding. On the contrary, much has happened in my absence from scribbling my thoughts and my feelings. One's journey does not have to be documented in daily baby steps. Transcribing my feelings in any form or fashion or timeframe is after all for me for right now. Fears and lack of a faith can too often cloud one's perspective, judgment, and progressive journey into the pull. Humans are just that and doubt and questioning is what we do.

Let us pick up with the colon cancer concerns. I did put the concerns in His hands. I cannot deny that I was still worried but less worried when I put Him in the driver's seat. The earliest doctor's appointment had been a long two months away. Finally. that day arrived with my symptoms still dogging me. Doctor Brown listened to my concerns and then scheduled a colonoscopy two days later. I was glad and concerned but believed He would do what was best for me. I prayed like I had never prayed before. Two days later I was prepped and prodded. The preliminary results in. Doctor Brown held back no punches. Three small polyps and two large polyps were removed. He felt the lab work would turn out good on them. He said there were no signs of cancer. Praise the Lord. The next week I received the news from the lab work. Everything was okay. I continued my nightly prayers and my morning devotion.

Serving the wine has taken on a new meaning for me too. I was asked to assist with communion, something that I have never ever done before in all my years on this earth. I did not even flinch when Judy asked me. I simply said okay. I am not sure who was more surprised, me or her. I opted for the wine part. I rehearsed my phrase, my prayer in the giving over and over so that I would not botch it. I didn't. This was another huge step for me, doing something like this in church. Church participation is indeed a new concept for me. Merely attending and remaining low profile had better served me forever. Boy, life can change when you least expect or in my case, had never seen it coming in the first place. I still credit Sammy and his uncanny way to get a point across to me. God is in charge though if truth be told.

I am leaping from one thing to the other but when you do not keep up your journal on a daily basis, this is what happens. We had a scheduled trip to Nashville. Hotel reservations already made. Tickets to several events already purchased. And then seemingly out of nowhere, a tropical depression formed and days before our planned departure, it became Hurricane Florence, a September cyclone with its sights on the Eastern Seaboard. We watched the weather reports, wondering with uncertainty if this was going to threaten Myrtle Beach or not. Eventually we received our answer less than a week before we were supposed to depart on our vacation. Florence quickly strengthened from a Cat 1 to Cat 4, with the South Carolina-North Carolina border in the crosshairs. Our worst nightmare became evident when the S.C. governor ordered a mandatory evacuation for Zones A, B and C on the coast. We reside in Zone B. The announcement came on Monday, effective to begin noon on Tuesday and we were scheduled to head toward Nashville on Sunday. What were we to do? Do we cancel the trip or go as planned?

I did something previously uncharacteristic for me. I prayed. I have not shared this prayer with anyone until now. I talked to God and told Him that I knew He could work miracles. I asked Him to work one with Hurricane Florence. My prayer was simple. I said, "God I know you have the power to dissipate this Cat 4 hurricane before it reaches our coast." Guess what? He did just that, bringing it to a screeching halt as a Cat 1 before it hit. We did evacuate as requested and we decided to go on to Abbeville for a few days before heading to Nashville, at the time uncertain of what may happen. Our house was spared, no damage and according to neighbors we did not even lose electricity.

Unfortunately, the storm stalled for days over the area, unleashing floods in N.C. and S.C. of epic proportions. So many people suffered from it. I prayed for them every night after the tragedy, to be with those coping and healing. Some might have prayed that the hurricane hit another location. I had not. I had simply asked for Him to dissipate the Cat 4 and He did. That was His doing, not mine. The rain did not stop though. Weeks later Hurricane Michael, a couple miles shy from being a Cat 5, slammed into the Florida Pan Handle, bringing a powerful storm surge and 165 mph winds. It devastated the Pan Handle. Miraculously, we were not in its path. My nightly prayer list was growing. So many people were suffering from these two storms.

In Nashville, six days into our vacation, we suffered a misunderstanding that turned into an ugly little feud that jeopardized the remainder of our vacation. Too often silly things can explode into majors between married couples. No amount of 'I'm sorry' seems to remedy them. I do not like arguments. I am too quick to want them to be over. I take the life is too short approach. It takes two to see it that way of course. I am not saying I am right by any stretch. Neither rights nor wrongs remedy situations like these. I am not patient and have a difficult time just putting it into cruise control and allowing it to run its course. I did my best, but my best usually just makes matters worse. So that night, I took a different approach and prayed that He might help us through this one. This was a first, me asking Him to help us fix it. I have learned even in the early going that merely asking does not always mean everything will be all right. So, what happened?

The next morning, I flipped over to my next marked devotion from Men of the Bible but before I began reading, I was compelled to backtrack. This thought to flip backwards in the pages came out of nowhere. Well, 'nowhere' is not exactly right. A greater power had taken the wheel again. This time He was redirecting my daily devotion. I was not sure why I was flipping back through the previously read pages, but I soon received my answer. Praise your wife was marked in the book. I read this and a calm came over me. I later shared it with her, and we emerged from our misunderstanding and hurtful feelings as we should. God is Good.

Trust, What a New Concept?

I know what you are probably thinking; this is going to be one of those 'me put my trust in the Lord lessons.' Maybe, maybe not. Well, I guess in a way it could be perceived as such. All things lead back to Him, I suppose. Listen to me. Revelations tend to have no boundaries. He can truly work in mysterious and miraculous ways. Boy howdy, am I the prime example, so it seems.

I received a call from a church member asking if I would become a trustee. Without thinking it through, I said okay. As soon as I had, I had a minor panic attack. What did I know about being a trustee? I had no clue what a trustee did. It was indeed another milestone for sure, but uncharted territory as well. This being pushed into the pull phenomena can be quite challenging and scary. What now? Should I Google trustee for the rest of the story to see what I had signed up for or should I ride it out and see where it takes me? I had more questions than I had answers for sure.

Okay, what now? I could not just renege on my commitment, could I? Following God can make life interesting, especially for an old dog like me. Desperate times require equally desperate measures. Possibly, that statement is a little over the top even for me. Uncertainty might be better put. I consulted Judy and she did not have definable answers. She suggested I talk with Gene, the son-in-law so I did. He had served as a trustee before and offered some insight into the responsibilities. There was no turning back or at least not an amicable way to bow out. A trustee I would be. I did not know it at the time that this was a three-year hitch. Locked and loaded I pushed onward; the first meeting scheduled not far in the forceable future. I found out that trustee's cycle out over the three-year stint, ensuring there is a combination of veterans and newbies at any given time. Still, I was venturing into uncharted waters.

I act like I am special, unique, or different by being selected to this task. What I am more concerned about is am I worthy to live up to the responsibilities and ownership of wearing the trustee badge. The mere implication of the title concerns me; 'trust' in doing what is right in church matters. I have always been a bench warmer, the guy sitting on the sidelines that never gets in the game. Now, I had gotten myself into being somewhat of a first stringer or maybe just a red shirt. Call me a rookie or a newbie, but commitments are commitments.

Being committed has not been one of my strong suits throughout life. I digress. I go back to high school when I tried out for football, basketball, and track. I never lasted more than a week at any of them. I did not like the rigorous schedule or puking, so I quit before giving any of them or me a fighting chance. This has been a theme in my life. I joined the junior band when I was in the sixth grade and was supposed to learn to play the coronet. I struggled through one year with that one. It did not hold my interest and I did not possess the discipline to learn to play it properly. I sort of partially blame my parents for my weakness. They worked the second shift and were not around most of the time. They did not instill in me to finish what I started. What makes me think this trustee stint is going to turn out any differently? God, you have got your work cut out for you, corralling this one. Herd me, the cat that I am.

I eventually sat in on the first trustee meeting, still unclear what my responsibilities were supposed to be. It was a bit informal and unstructured for my liking. I have worked a career in quality assurance in the manufacturing world. Our meetings had an agenda and followed that agenda with explicit protocol. Before retiring in 2015 I oversaw the facility's document control system and was also in charge of the auditing system, everything with checks and balances. There was no 'how to be a trustee' manual offered. There was no list of responsibilities. I did not even understand most of the items the group was discussing or voting on. Those of us who were new, were not introduced, nor were those who were not new introduced. I had not signed up for this and didn't like it from the get-go. After that first meeting I was ready to bail. Commitment, my weakness was living large. Against my better judgment, I talked myself into to giving it another try. We only met quarterly after all. How bad could that be?

After nearly a year, I am still a trustee and we now meet monthly. I am feeling better about the responsibilities for funds and the church grounds and all that go into decisions concerning approving money to be used for this and that. God had His plan. I should have gotten that memo in the beginning. He was not going to allow me to bow out when it came to something important as serving Him. My bad, I should have reached out to Him a lifetime ago. Rebellious, selfish, destructive, and bulletproof did not play into my plans and the pathetic direction I had chosen. God stuck to his guns apparently, knowing what I didn't. For whatever reason, one that only He knows, there is some purpose for me being such a late bloomer. He sure did protect me more times than I can count when my life could have come to an end or had a much more disastrous outcome. Nope. I am not second guessing or questioning anything. I am just going with the flow, with the pull and I will go where it takes me, where He leads me.

Wrestling with It

Kind of like an addict, sometimes you must admit you have a problem. No, I am not on drugs and I have no addiction to alcohol. In my day I was wild and crazy but now older and wiser I have given up most of my craziness. Like being at an AA meeting, I begin by saying, 'Hi. I am Tom and I watch the WWE, professional wrestling if one can consider it professional from a sports perspective. Allow me to further clarify. I have never attended an AA meeting and I am not one of those who believe wrestling is real. I get it. To me it is like watching a soap opera or a television series or movie. There are bad guys scripted and pitted against good guys. Sometimes the good guys win. Often the bad guys do, all for the entertainment factor.

For the record, I have only attended one live wrestling match in my entire life. It would have been in the late seventies, back in the day of the Four Horsemen, Dusty Rhodes, Magnum T.A., Superstar Billy Graham and an assortment of masked heroes and villains. I think I watched the crowd at the Greenwood, S.C. Civic Center as much as I watched the action in the squared circle. There were those around me who were true believers. Screaming for their favorites, while others were crying, and I do mean tears flowing over their heroes being supposedly decimated in the ring. The handful of guys that had invited me was totally into it as well.

True believers, everyone had to believe in something I suppose. We all have ours. Yep, I still watch wrestling. I record it now on the DVR and skim through the sometimes three hour televised events. If anything, it has gotten more theatrical, scripted, and filled with trash talking and challenges. One episode hit home though. This one did not seem to be scripted. Well, maybe it was for television, but I genuinely believe that the unfortunate circumstances the wrestler found himself in were real. This guy had pleased and angered fans from both sides of the aisle. For stints he would be portrayed as the unlikable bad guy and then as scripted for so many, he would transform from villain to hero. He was a top name, big draw. Like him or not, he was a main player in wrestling game.

Not unlike any start to a Monday Night Raw episode, some wrestler or wrestlers would start the episode taking center stage with a microphone and profess what he or she intended to do to who and when. Someone would have done someone else wrong or there would be a championship belt in someone's sight. Many times, I will fast forward through these smack talk segments. I am not sure why I didn't tonight, but I am glad I didn't. Make believe can often mimic reality. This one would be as real as they get and ended up hitting awfully close to home, proving lessons don't always come from scripture or devotional studies.

Professional wrestler, performer, Roman Reigns walked the runway to his entrance music. The screen flashed his mantra, 'The Roman Empire.' Microphone in hand he entered the ring to the boos and dismay of the crowd. Roman was currently on the bad apple list, a villain and despised personality. In wrestling, the popularity, good or bad guy, is rated by the decimal meter, loudness in cheers or jeers setting the tone for popularity and success. No PR is bad PR. I did not press the fast forward and prepared for the smack talk. I, like the crowd, had not been prepared for the revelation and personal journey of a man who now introduced himself as Leati Joseph Anoa'I, Joe being his real name, Not Roman. It went like this.

"My real name is Joe, and I've been living with leukemia for 11 years," Anoa'i said to the crowd at Dunkin' Donuts Center in Providence, Rhode Island. "And, unfortunately, it's back. And because the leukemia is back, I cannot fulfill my role -- I can't be that fighting champion -- and I'm going to have to relinquish the Universal championship... I want to make one thing clear: By no means is this a retirement speech. Because after I'm done whipping leukemia's ass once again, I'm coming back home."

After the announcement, the WWE sent out a news release with a few additional details on Anoa'i's condition.

"Tonight, on Monday Night Raw, Roman Reigns [a.k.a. Joe Anoa'i] announced that he is relinquishing the WWE Universal championship and taking a leave of absence from WWE as he once

122

again fights leukemia, which had been in remission since late 2008," the WWE said in the statement. "Reigns is taking his battle with leukemia public in an effort to raise awareness and funds for research in order to advance cures for the disease."

Anoa'i last performed in a WWE ring Oct. 15, in the main event of Monday Night Raw. It's unclear when Anoa'i received the diagnosis that his leukemia had returned.

Anoa'i, 33, played college football for Georgia Tech and attempted to play for both the Minnesota Vikings and Jacksonville Jaguars. He then played a season in the Canadian Football League and retired from football in 2008. He ultimately signed with the WWE in 2010, debuted onscreen for the company in late 2012 and has become one of the most recognizable performers in the WWE.

After making his announcement, Reigns laid down the title belt in the ring and was then embraced at the top of the entrance ramp by teammates and close friends Dean Ambrose and Seth Rollins. To eliminate any doubt as to the veracity of Reigns' condition, and whether it was simply a fictional move for the show rather than a real circumstance, WWE commentator Michael Cole made a statement once the show returned from commercial break.

"We come out here every Monday night to entertain. That's what we all do," Cole said to the TV audience. "We live in this alternate reality sometimes, and I think we all forget that we're real people. And the superstars in the locker room are real people, and reality came up here and bit us tonight. And all I want to say is prayers are with you, brother, go get 'em."

Anoa'i was scheduled to perform in a three-way match against Brock Lesnar and Braun Strowman in a headlining match at the WWE's Crown Jewel show Nov. 2, which had been scheduled to take place in Riyadh, Saudi Arabia; WWE announced later in Monday's broadcast that Strowman and Lesnar would go one-on-one at Crown Jewel to determine a new champion. The WWE has said it is monitoring developments in Saudi Arabia concerning the country's alleged role in the death of journalist Jamal Khashoggi.

This revelation by Roman, 'Joe', as I said, hit too close to home. The loss of Sammy Cannon flooded my heart and my head. He had put up a valiant fight against leukemia as well, losing his battle. I felt for Roman and what might be ahead for him. Fake and theatrical just reached new heights. There would have probably been a time that this confession would not have resonated so for me. Then again, I can get quite emotional to this sort of stuff. No denying it, it had struck a chord. I found myself praying for Roman and his family. Me, praying for a make-believe entertainer, a wrestler, but a man in need of our prayers.

The movie, Indivisible, struck a nerve with me as well. We try to pick movies with a message when we do go to the movies. This one fit that bill, similarities with losing family, mood, and depression. Quick synopsis, fresh out of the seminary and basic training, Army chaplain, Darren Turner ends up in Iraq, leaving his wife and three young children. The harsh realities of a brutal war take its toll on him, his battalion and eventually disconnect him from his family upon his return. He and his wife are faced with just how badly they are willing to fight and save their marriage. So many face this challenge, even in the smallest of arenas. Keeping the faith in God ensures that things work out for the best. This is one of those must-see movies.

All Saints day snuck up on me as well, still mourning the loss of Cuz. This pull thing just keeps hitting from every possible direction. Everything tends to be up close and personal, relevant so it seems in God's guiding hands. Lessons are around every corner if you open your heart and embrace them. It is becoming easier for me to recognize them, understand them and appreciate them. It is funny how that has happened in such a short time. Well, sixty-five years in the making isn't exactly short if you really put it in perspective. Proves that it is never too late. I am a testament to that fact, so it seems. I still have a long journey ahead, but I am staying the course.

Devotion for the day: Second Chances: 2 Kings 5:11 – summary, you may have really messed up your past life of faith, but you do not have to live in the past. God believes in second chances.

I cannot add much more to that. Second chances and I have certainly messed up plenty during a life done my way, come hell, or high water. Back then I never learned from my mistakes. I tended to repeat them, and they ended with the same results. Nothing good and people harmed by my reckless and selfish behavior.

To Forgive or Not Forgive

Never by just mere chance, He makes sure of that. My devotion reading this AM was from Philemon 1:10-12 titled To Forgive or Not Forgive. It always gives a modern example and then the Biblical reference. In summary it read: Do we forgive and restore, or do we withhold forgiveness and allow the relationship to fester and die?

Boy, what powerful words these were. It finishes with this lesson: Understanding God's grace and forgiveness is the key to forgiving those who have hurt us. When we extend forgiveness to those who need it, we free them to realize what God intends for them.

I guess in general I have been a forgiving person. I despise conflict and bickering. Nope, I am not perfect by a long shot and certainly not without fault in these matters. I can get caught up in these as easy as the next person, but it does not mean I have to like it. I lean toward saying I am sorry for what I did or said, hopeful that the one I offended forgives me. I cannot control it from the other side. Will the person accept my apology and forgive me? That festering thing again just never sets well with me. It is like having a gnawing heartburn or a bad case of indigestion. It can often hurt and refuse to go away if both parties do not seek the same cure and do it quickly. It is often a bitter pill to swallow, a person saying I am sorry or the other forgiving that person. Feelings hurt are often tough to mend. Wallowing in it never helps. It is back to that 'life is already too short' thing to waste valuable time. Our next second, minute, day, week, month, or year is not guaranteed. One blink and anything can come to a tragic ending. Cherish what you have if you can muster up the forgiveness.

Here is another of my morning devotions: Zephaniah 3:17, God will not give you up. Summary, God does not cut us loose when we do not do as He wishes. He forgives us and sticks to the plan He has for us.

If God can forgive us, why do we struggle with forgiving one another? We all have our moments. We are human after all and certainly not perfect. We will always say or do something that does not set well with others. Taking every little thing said or done too personally will ruin the best relationship or friendship. So, how do we better ourselves? How do we turn a cheek and man or woman up and say I am sorry, or I forgive you? Nothing is ever easy where we humans are concerned. Our world constantly comes with challenges and consequences based on the decisions we make, good or poor ones. Taking the high road seems to be the best solution if you really think about it. Why did so many of us lean toward prolonging the inevitable? Wouldn't it be so much easier if we chose the shortcut instead of the long route? Forgiving saves valuable time. Love and live. This does not come easy for me, quoting Biblical terms, but I do understand the relevance, still in the pull.

Valuable lessons can still be difficult. Old habits tend to raise their ugly heads as well. The evil doer battling all of us is always watchful, looking for any opening to persuade us to venture into the dark side, to backslide and undo good things we have spent valuable time alleviating. I suffer and succumb to those hiccups as much as the next person. Too often I never see them coming until they have already arrived and then it is too late to undo what has been done. I did not take my devotional book on a Columbia trip recently, figuring skipping one day would not hurt. By doing so I did not begin my morning by re-reading the chapter about respecting your wife before reading my daily one. I backslid and for that I am terribly sorry. I said I was sorry when sorry was not nearly enough. I said I love you when just saying it was not nearly enough either. Life is still a give and take world. Apologizing and forgiving go hand in hand. One does not work without the other. Allowing it to fester serves absolutely no purpose. Life's lessons continue within the power of the pull. I stumble. I fall. I try to learn from my weaknesses. Sometimes I am successful. Sometimes I am not. I know I am trying to do better, be better but it is not easy undoing a lifetime of doing the absolute opposite.

Holding onto the Reins

Sometimes life manages to toss you some feel good nuggets. This is one of those times. Joe surfaced once again. Prayer and belief in God do work. Here is more proof. This is Roman Reigns, the Wrestler, announcement about leukemia 4 months later

WWE star Roman Reigns, who's real name is Joe Anoa'i, announced Monday night that his leukemia is in remission and that he intends to return to ring action.
Reigns, 33, stepped away from the WWE in October by announcing that, 11 years after he had first battled leukemia, the disease had returned. He vacated the WWE Universal championship at that time and stepped away from the limelight to fight the disease.

As the "Monday Night Raw" crowd at the State Farm Arena in Atlanta cheered him on, Reigns walked to the ring, did a lap to greet the fans at ringside, and then spoke to the WWE crowd for the first time in four months:

After speaking about his faith in God, the tremendous outreach from WWE fans and the prayers and messages shared over the past few months, Reigns revealed an update on his condition. "The good news is, I'm in remission, y'all," Reigns said. "With that being said, the big dog is back."

"I missed y'all. There is no other job like this," Reigns said. "There's no other fan base like you guys."

I think back to Sammy again, his battle with leukemia ending in death and me losing my best friend. I realize we have no control over these situations and merely praying for better outcomes do not make them go the way we want them to go. Why Roman and not Sammy? I know it is not my place to question His will. I get it. His plan opened me up to accepting Him in Sammy's case. While accepting losing Sammy to get here is still tough, I am trying to be a better person so that Sammy's loss does not go in vain.

This takes me back to the up and down relationship with one of my golf buddies and coworkers, Carl. He and I leaned on one another while Sammy and his friend Joe battled cancer. I lost one brother and gained another in the process. We had experienced petty differences in the past, many to do with those golf misunderstandings. Sadly, forgive and forget, apologies were hard to swallow. Being pigheaded is not pretty. Carl found himself feuding with another coworker, one he had befriended for fifteen years. And yes, golf situations had come into play. His friend was struggling with demons, personal and work related and vented taking it out on Carl or at least in a manner Carl did not appreciate. We chatted about it and I assumed the unlikely role of a counselor. I asked Carl if a fifteen-year friendship was worth losing over something that in the big picture did not really mean much. His friend needed a friend. At his speed, no right or wrong way to get there, they settled their differences. I take no credit in this. Powers greater than I guided everyone through the forgiving, forgetting, and healing process. Did either ask God to intervene? That is between them and the Man in charge.

Life can come at you in a confusing and often jumbled mess. After quite a long time and seemingly out of nowhere, Sammy visited me in another dream. Wacky dreams are sometimes just that and hard to follow and often just as difficult to decipher. When it comes to Cuz making an appearance, I always pay close attention and try to learn something from them though. So here goes the latest.

The dream scene opens with this secret door off the garage at Sammy and Judy's house, one I certainly have never seen before. So, here we go, off on one of those magical Cuz journeys so it seems. He motions for me to follow him. We enter this mysterious portal in his garage, and I find myself viewing some sort of Sammy tribute room of his life with Judy. There are all these keepsake viewing windows. I peer inside them as encouraged by Cuz. Each room is animated and is of memorable moments in their lives. After viewing several, another doorway led to a fireplace, a fire pit and grill. It was outdoors, his sanctuary. Behind another door is a full kitchen and yet another had a secluded bedroom. This is apparently Sammy's hidden world after leaving ours. There was no golf, no cold beer or lost

Sammy articles as what were experienced in a real lifetime with him. His world was complete. He seemed content and excited to share these wonders with me. I was just so glad to see him and be around him, if only in a vivid dream. I woke and cherished these priceless details, wasting no time scribing them down before I forgot them. I needed this visit. God is indeed Good and knows what we need and when we need it.

Answered prayers fall into place: Friend and golfing bud Ed has a long-awaited surgery that will hopefully reconcile some of his medical issues. New West Virginia friend and snowbird Tom Marsh tells me about his wife Laura's lymphoma scare, adding it had been in remission. March 6, 2019, I attended my very first Ash Wednesday service at age almost 66. Man, it is crazy. My life is filled with faith changing events.

Speaking of faith and God's unique way to deliver the message, I had been reviewing this chapter earlier today, many months after I had written it. During dinner, Judy and I dining in the sunroom as we usually do, I randomly selected a prerecorded movie titled Forever My Girl. The plot, Liam Page is a county music superstar who left his bride Josie at the altar to pursue fame and fortune. Page never got over Josie, his one true love, or forgot his Southern roots in the small town where he was born and raised. Now he must unexpectedly face the consequences of his actions when he returns to his hometown for the funeral of his best friend from high school.

Liam's dad is a preacher. The two have not spoken much since he left, and there are a lot of hard feelings between them and the town folk, against Liam for what he did eight years ago. In one of the hometown opening scenes upon his return his dad is delivering the message during a Sunday sermon that everyone deserves mercy and forgiveness. He tells the congregation that the scripture says for forgiveness for love in all man you must have the capacity to forgive. He continues saying it sounds so easy in theory, doesn't it but it is profoundly difficult. In this church he tells them that we have always tried to practice forgiveness. Today let's try to forgive those that have hurt us and move forward. And if we can truly forgive, we can truly be accepted.

No spoiler alert: this ended up being an inspiring movie. I highly recommend it. It will indeed open your eyes to believing and having faith that all things happen for a reason. In the end though, forgiveness will set you free. Mere chance tuning into this movie today on a Sunday afternoon, I don't think so.

Snowbirds and Seagulls

Sounds like a play or a movie or something, doesn't it? The program was started by our church many years ago to welcome travelers during the winter to the Grand Strand. Many migrate to Myrtle Beach for an extended stay, most staying for months enjoying the warmer beach weather. Thusly, these migrating travelers have earned the name of snowbirds. The locals are dubbed the seagulls. The premise of the program is to offer fellowship and worship for those vacationing away from home. Included are eight Tuesdays of golf during the Jan-Feb months, a mix and match captain's choice on various courses with discount rates offered. Snowbirds are encouraged to attend regular church services and a special Monday night service is held for the snowbirds in our chapel. On Thursdays from January through March there is a program in our fellowship hall at 11:15, scheduled entertainment and a meal. It was our first year attending as seagulls because now we could attend since I had fully retired in 2018. Our church, the First United Methodist, is called 'The church with a heart in the heart of Myrtle Beach.' It is located directly across from what used to be the multistory pavilion parking garage.

March 14, 2019, we had a wonderful Snowbirds and Seagulls Thursday program. A mix up ended with two speakers being scheduled for the same date, what a blessed mistake. The gentlemen knew each other. The first to speak was a local, combo of songwriter-singer-speaker. Through speech and song, he gave his testimony and journey. Years ago, he had been diagnosed with stage four cancer. He prayed that God would cure him and believed He would. If He did not, he was ready for the next journey to heaven. Aggressive chemo and prayers cured him. He had been singing since he was eight and made his survival part of his ministry, visiting nursing homes, caregivers, and churches. Recently he had a doctor's appointment and there still was no sign of the cancer, but the doctor told him he needed to lose weight as he laughed.

The second gentleman, a local sort of, living in the area since he was five, now in his sixties or seventies, was a motivational speaker as well. He had first found God when he was forty, sound familiar. My awakening came nearly twenty-five years after his. He shared his stories and miracles since finding the Lord. This might have been the best and most uplifting program we have attended in the three-month long Snowbirds and Seagulls Thursdays. I met a new brother during one of the golf outings, Tom Marsh from West Virginia, a retired Baptist preacher. He and I hit it off like we had known each other forever. He is featured numerous times in my book, The Endless Mulligan. He gave me plenty of ammunition for stories on the links. Love this man. He had been trying to talk his wife Laura into them moving here full time. She had previously told me Tom could move and she would miss him. Today Tom told me she was considering coming here six months instead of three. I told him I would keep working on her.

Now this brings me to my next revelation. I do not often dream (or am visited by Sammy much lately) but when I am, I try my best to remember the experience. Last night I had the pleasure of his company once again. We (Judy and I) were at their home in Greenwood. Cuz was sitting in his familiar recliner with his blanky pulled over his lap. He told us that his Judy was not there. She had moved to Abbeville (all true now since his death). She had in recent months sold their home and had moved to Abbeville in rental property while waiting to build a new house. In the dream Sammy said he was glad she had moved on without him. He said he had moved on also. In the dream I had brought Cuz two pairs of golf knickers and matching accessories. One pair of knickers was a bright lime green with flowery knee-high socks and a matching sweater vest. The other ensemble was just as gaudy. Cuz quickly told me he was not going to wear them. A few minutes later he said he would. My Judy pointed out that the second set was too large, Cuz now being too frail for them to fit. That's it. That's all I remember. What this did bring back though was the last time I saw Sammy before he died. It was a shortened one day visit with him at their home in Greenwood. We had planned a longer stay but doctors had insisted he move closer to the hospital in Greenville-Spartanburg, so they were moving in with his twin sister, Susan, who lived in the immediate area. Sammy had been sitting in that chair with his blanky looking frail. I helped load their things and him in the car the next morning, a tough goodbye, not knowing that would be the last time I would see him.

Now I have never been one to try to interpret a dream, that is until Cuz passed, and his death so dramatically touched my humble life. Sammy came to me after the church program, no doubt in my mind. He was telling me that it was okay that Judy had sold their home and had moved on, because he had started his new life over year ago after his death. He, finally agreeing to wear the gaudy lime knickers was his way of saying that clothing really holds no great significance once you have reached your heavenly status. He merely pacified me, knowing that if I continued on my path, it wouldn't matter to me either. Pastor Buddy told me there is no right or wrong way to yield to the pull and no time frame to get there. Funny, after my morning devotion and after my shower, lyrics from Jerry Reed's signature song from Smokey and the Bandit was humming in my head; 'There's a long way to go and short time to get there.' Thank you Cuz for that wonderful dreamtime visit once again.

Just two weeks before Sammy's birthday, the second since he died, I had another one of those wacky dreams. I knew the time reference to his birthday because my Judy had informed me that his Judy would be heading to Hilton Head to celebrate Sammy's birthday with his twin sister Susan. I have often stated that some of my best ideas for writing topics come to me in dreams. When a humdinger invades my nighttime, I do my absolute best to retain it. I have developed a method for continuously replaying the dream throughout the night and then I make note of it once morning arrives. Often these are converted into a short story or maybe even a novel. This one just seemed appropriate to include in my scribbling now. Over the next few nights, while lying in bed, I advanced the narrative for the story in my head as if led to do it. Here is my completed short as brought to me by powers only One can be responsible to inspire me. I titled it Wishful Dreaming.

Wishful Dreaming

Sandy wiped the grogginess from her crusted eyes. The room, her bedroom, felt oddly different. The light was all wrong for her typical morning wakeup. She attempted to shake the cobwebs from her head, reassessing her surroundings. No denying it, something was off. A mixture of fog and brilliant light contributed to her disorientation. Sandy, not realizing she had risen from bed, now stood in the nothingness, a dreamlike state at best.

"Welcome Sandra. Be not afraid."

"Who are you? Where are you? Where am I?"

"Not important, Sandra."

"Sure, they are important, important to me. I have a right to know unless this is just a silly dream. If it is not a dream and instead some sort of weird alien abduction, then I am ready to return home."

"And return you shall but you must choose one item, an item important to you."

"Who are you and what is this game you are promoting?"

"One item, Sandra. Do this for me, for you."

The episode, dream or whatever it had been, began to fade for Sandra.

Cal blinked once then twice. He yawned, stretched, and rubbed his eyes but it did not help. He had fallen asleep on the sofa as he often did now, but the usual sound of the television blaring was not evident. Nothing seemed normal. He stood but even standing seemed wrong. His den, where was his den? Crazy, just all too crazy he thought. Living alone, sometimes life could just seem a bit too spooky.

"Welcome Calvin. Be not afraid."

"That's easy for you to say, whoever you are and wherever you are hiding."

"Neither is important."

"I reckon it might be, a stranger being inside my house, sneaking up on a helpless old man while he's sleeping. If you are out to rob me, just take whatever you want. I don't have much, nothing worth me dying over."

"I mean you no harm, Calvin. Choose an item that is important to you."

"What, and then hand it over to you? Just take what you want and leave."

"One item, Calvin. Do this for me, for you."

Everything began to fade and return to normal. Normal as life could be anyway in Calvin's life.

Bill sensed he was not alone. Fearing a home invasion, he considered arming himself and readying to do battle. Nobody trespassed on his property, especially inside his house, and did so without walking into a buzz saw. He would not go down without taking the intruder with him. The room did not feel right. It was murky swirled with bright lights, maybe the intruder's flashlight.

"Welcome William. Be not afraid."

"Whoa. Nobody calls me William. Friend or foe and you better choose wisely."

"Fear not. You have but one mission William. Choose an item that is important to you. Do this for me, for you."

"Right and then you'll steal me blind, won't you?"

Bill stood on wobbly legs, the stranger no longer feeling to be nearby.

Sandra sat on the side of her bed, unsure how to react to what had just happened, if it had really happened. Yet, she felt a sudden urgency to abide by the stranger's request. The room appeared as it always appeared. Nothing in her bedroom was out of place but normal did not seem quite normal. Choose an item that is important to me the voice had instructed her. What did this really mean? Why did doing this seem so important? Choose something of importance. It was almost like playing the 'what if game.' What if your house was on fire and you only had time to take one item and flee for your life? What would she take? She lived alone and had no pets. What would she choose? Pretending as if she did not have a moment to spare, she picked her item.

Cal did not like this. He did not like this one little bit. What had just happened? Had it all been just a crazy dream brought on by him gorging too late on peanut butter and vanilla wafers? It had felt like a dream but not really. So, what did that mean? Choose something important the voice had said. He did not own anything important. What had been important to him forever no longer existed. Life in general just was not that important. A grown man spending his nights sleeping on the sofa summed up his life in a nutshell. Still, what that voice had said dogged him something terrible. Pick something that meant something to him, something of importance. What did he have to pick from in his sorry existence? That very second, he knew, and he placed his hand on what meant the most to him.

Bill swore out loud. This was such a crock what had just happened. Nobody came uninvited inside his house. Nobody! And now this home invader had just up and vanished after demanding that he select his most prize possession. Pick it, right? Anything worth cherishing was worth stealing and this culprit had some nerve conning him to boot. He would choose all right. He would make this scoundrel regret ever asking him. Bill knew exactly the appropriate item to flaunt the importance of selecting. Messing with him in his house had been a huge mistake. It came with consequences. Bring it on. I got your important item for me and for you.

"Sandra, you have chosen."

Sandy found herself back in that strange existence, the nothing world of fog and light. No matter how hard she focused the scene before her remained the same. The bodiless voice surrounded her, echoed within her, and shadowed her with a calming affect.

"Sandra. explain your choice of importance for you, for me."

"I chose my laptop computer. It holds everything dear to me. Photographs and videos of my children, their spouses, my grandchildren and their spouses, my great grandchildren and closest friends and relatives for they are my life."

"Explain, Sandra for you, for me."

"You see, I escaped an abusive relationship more years ago than I care to remember. We were so young when we married. I had not known my husband very long, already with child and forced to do what was supposed to be the right thing to do. Quickly I learned how bad decisions can offer worse horrors. This man, my husband, was an abusive terror to me and my unborn child. Four children later nothing changed. He hurt me. He hurt my children verbally and physically. One day I prayed to God to please let it end by whatever means He saw fit. My husband shortly thereafter attacked a neighbor beating him within an inch of his life and set the poor family's home on fire. He was sentenced to a long stay in prison where he died at the hands of another inmate. God answered my prayers for me and my children. Good memories are inside that laptop."

Calvin again found himself in the dreamlike state. He had no memory of arriving here again. Magically so, here he was in the mist and bright light, neither offering a clue of his whereabouts. He said nothing and simply waited for whoever brought him here to make the first move. He did not have long to wait.

"Calvin. You have chosen."

"I reckon I did. It wasn't that tough. I don't really own anything that important except for this."

"Explain Calvin, for you, for me."

"My wife Eleanor died of that awful Alzheimer's last year. That is the cruelest of all diseases by my reckoning. We had been married for almost fifty-seven years. Next month would have been our fifty-seventh. I cannot even sleep in our bed anymore. She died in that bed, a bed we shared, a life of love everlasting. Don't get me wrong, we had a wonderful life, even through the hard times when her mind was going. That was the hardest though when she did not know I was her husband. She could not help it. I certainly did not hold it against her. I loved that woman with all my heart. It has been tough her not being here. If not for the Good Book, her Bible, I do not know what I would have done. You see, she always wrote her thoughts in that Bible after reading the scripture or after God touched her in some way that made her relate to the written words. I sit alone every night and read her words and those of the Good Book until it comforts me. Then I turn on that TV for noise and fall asleep on the couch when my heart and mind gives into it. This Bible, her Bible is my most important possession. I draw comfort from it every single day. I begin my mornings reading my devotion from it and it lays me down to sleep every single night, for this I know."

Bill became edgy then furious, sensing the home invader had again trespassed in the world that belonged solely to him. He was ready this time. Tell me to pick something important so you can snatch it up. I don't think so. Smoke and mirrors, trick or treat, face me like a man whoever you are.

"William, you have chosen."

"Damn right I have chosen. This isn't my first rodeo."

"Explain William, for you, for me."

"This country is going to hell in a hand basket. I saw it coming years ago and I prepared for it. I have the means to defend myself and the will to outlast it. Bring it on. I do not trust anyone, especially anybody associated with government. They want to steal my rights, take my guns, and con me into being dependent on them. I don't need anybody. I can take care of myself. I am just mere steps from dropping off the grid all together. Now I will be the first to admit that I'm not the Godliest of men, but I know right from wrong. It is just plain wrong what a handful are trying to do to us. They took God out of the schools. They want to take God out of the pledge for which we stand and now they want to kill babies even after they have been born. This same scum does not mind spending money stamped with 'In God We Trust' though. Heck, they want to take the money from those who earned it fair and square and give it to those who haven't hit a lick of work or even worse, those crossing our border illegally. Where is God? Why is he allowing this to even happen? This gun I have in my hand is what I picked. It is an equalizer, my protection to keep them out and don't think I won't use it. Sometimes God needs help to make things right for us honest hard-working folks."

"Sandra, you have indeed suffered, and you have chosen what you cherish most, family and the friends you love. You prayed and asked for help because you believe in the power of prayer and in the One that answers those prayers. You will not need that device. Take my hand, Sandra. Jesus loves you, this I know."

"Calvin, you have indeed lost the one who meant so much to you. From here, you have learned much. Take my hand, Calvin, for the Bible tells me so."

"William, you have much hatred and distrust in your life, but you recognize the power. Yes, you have many questions and concerns and much yet to experience. It is not your time but remember, yes, Jesus loves you. He who died; heaven's gate to open wide. He will wash away your sin; let His little child come in. Trust in Him, William and we will talk again.

Jesus loves me! This I know,
For the Bible tells me so;
Little ones to Him belong,
They are weak but He is strong.
Yes, Jesus loves me!
Yes, Jesus loves me!
Yes, Jesus loves me!
The Bible tells me so.

Jesus loves me! He who died,
Heaven's gate to open wide;
He will wash away my sin,
Let His little child come in.
Yes, Jesus loves me!
Yes, Jesus loves me!
Yes, Jesus loves me!

The Bible tells me so.

Jesus loves me! loves me still,
When I'm very weak and ill;
From His shining throne on high,
Comes to watch me where I lie.
Yes, Jesus loves me!
Yes, Jesus loves me!

Yes, Jesus loves me!
The Bible tells me so.

Jesus loves me! He will stay,
Close beside me all the way;
He's prepared a home for me,
And some day His face I'll see.
Yes, Jesus loves me!
Yes, Jesus loves me!
Yes, Jesus loves me!
The Bible tells me so

Sometimes devotion materializes from unlikely places. You do not have to crack open the Bible or read from a specific text. Take it where you can get it and cherish the delivery. Wishful Dreaming clung vividly in my head, playing it over and over until I awakened to the premise of the lesson. It's all-in understanding what is truly important and not believing in that which isn't. Each person must arrive and derive at their own pace. It does not matter how you get there or how long it takes you to get there. God will wait until you find the way. The pull is all powerful.

A Holy Land Experience

Many people dream of going to Jerusalem, visiting the land where Jesus walked and had spread the Word. Travel is no cheap. There are plenty of tours and offers out there though. Our church had planned several such annual excursions. Plane travel is difficult for Judy because she suffers from excruciating ear pain due to the altitude variances in flying. There is always that uncertainty and uneasiness traveling out of the country, especially in or through regions of the world where they hate America. Is the ultimate experience worth it? Anyone who has done it will say absolutely. Still, we struggle with committing to the experience. So, what do you do if you cannot quite muster the gumption to take the plunge?

First of all, I must disclaim that this is not an info commercial. Orlando offers an alternative and air travel is not necessarily required. There is a Disney like theme park geared to the Holy Land. It is a replica of the town on a smaller scale, a world designed to offer the experience without leaving home so to speak. For us it is not much more than an eight-hour drive, excluding food and rest stops. Settled, we were going to take this approach instead of journeying to the real deal. Online I purchased ticket vouchers at a cost of $50 each, much cheaper than Disney or Universal. And we could use them anytime within the next twelve months. Seemed like a no brainer. We scheduled a time and reserved a stay at a nearby hotel. We decided to drive and do a one night stop over in St. Augustine on the way down and would stop for a couple nights in Savannah on the way back, family R&R, spending three nights in Orlando.

The first leg of our journey was literally a wash out, raining the entire time we were in the oldest city in America. It ended up being just a stop to sleep and eat. We then took the slow boat route along the scenic coastal highway until we arrived in Daytona. From there we traveled the backroads through some nostalgic communities on our way to Orlando. A pleasant trek until we arrived at the chaotic travel and ever-changing infrastructure of Orlando. Prayers were in abundant engagement as we navigated the construction laden interstate. Unexpected lane changes certainly introduced its fair share of challenges. When we did finally arrive at our hotel, we pleasantly discovered that we were mere minutes away from the Holy Land theme park. All that remained, pick the best day to attend.

We chose our day and we arrived early, the parking lot with few cars yet. This was not going to be the Disney wild and crazy experience, so it seemed. We were wondering if all the hype for the Holy Land Experience had been highly overrated and exaggerated. A few cars began trickling into the parking lot. Gates would not open until 10 and would close around 6, certainly not a long time on the Disney and Universal grand scale of things to take it all in. TBD if we had chosen a valid substitute for the real deal. We were experiencing a bit of excitement mingled with a smidgen of apprehension. In mere minutes we would have our answer. More cars arrived. The parking lot resembled something more like one you would see at a Wal-Mart, not a theme park.

Open for business, we entered the park, having already scanned the park's brochure to formulate a plan to ensure we got our money's worth in the allotted timeframe. We found ourselves in a Jesus like setting, the surroundings seemingly a replica of ancient times. Again, we had nothing to compare it to the real experience, did we? We were pleasantly surprised though. The live shows and events, based on Biblical scripture had a natural flow to it throughout the park, allowing us to move from the completion of one to the beginning of the next, no fighting crowds and lines. Each segment was spot on as I could tell but then I am a newbie at this. Judy was fascinated by the presentations. Some scenes were disturbing because as they say, it is what it was, but most were quite uplifting.

This was so laid back from any theme park we had ever visited. You either received a message or a blessing or both. It had been one hundred dollars well spent. We met nothing but nice park attendants and equally as nice visitors. Tranquility prevailed. One lady told us her family returned quarterly because the theme changed to mimic Biblical times and scriptures throughout the year. No doubt, this would not be ourt last visit. No spoilers here; you need to come and see for yourself, experience it, and determine if it checked all the boxes for you. We saw almost everything in the time allotted, missing only a couple of venues. We did not miss any of the live shows though.

Since our trip to Orlando, we also took a bus trip to Kentucky and visited the Ark and the Creation Museum. Both blew us away. It is wonderful to think that Godly concepts and experiences are alive and well. We all need this even if we did not think we could be inspired. It gives one earlier in the pull a new appreciation of what was sacrificed for us. Powers beyond our imaginations created a world and shaped it, provided for us, and led the people to a promise land of epic proportions. God can end this and take it away as easily as he created it. Love and worship him, love it, and live life as He would wish us to for the remaining days we have on this wonderful earth.

Thank You God for a Sunny, Sonny Sunday

Sonny Clardy, a native of Myrtle Beach and owner of Reflections Assisted Living, has enjoyed singing spiritual and gospel songs for over forty years, for which he has many recordings. He has sung in local churches, for FUMC Sunday School classes, and has provided programs for the Snowbirds and Seagulls each year.

We also had a special pre-service treat in the chapel on Palm Sunday. Sonny began the program by saying he missed Big Tom not being here and just how much he loved and respected him. Tom Britain, in his nineties, is a retired pastor, a man loved by all. He said he first met Tom many years ago when his father died. Sonny grew up as a Baptist. Big Tom, a Methodist minister, was the first person to drop by and pay his condolences to Sonny's mother.

During the Snowbird and Seagulls event Sonny blended in inspirational and personal experiences with the songs he sang. Many he had written himself. He looked for amen's from the congregation, saying Baptist say amen a lot. Sonny had been diagnosed with advanced cancer twenty some odd years ago. The odds were not in his favor. He told how a group of various preachers gathered around him and prayed for him. He was lifted and told his wife everything was going to be all right. It might be a long tough road, but he put his faith in the Lord's healing hands. Eventually he licked it with all the prayers and with God's help. One story he told had to do with one of Reflections' tenants. The lady was not there long before passing, Sonny recalled how this wonderful woman would come to his house at least once a week and pray for him to be cured of the cancer. What he did not know he learned before she passed while in his facility. She told him she came more often than once a week and would stand on his porch and pray for him. The powers of prayers are not always done with you knowing it.

One song he sang titled Reflections was a two part one he had written about a 94-year-old woman and 98-year-old man who had died at Reflections. Both lives had touched him. He also tossed out thanks to the caregivers. They are rare and hard to find and bless those who are suffering with their unconditional love and care. Obviously, this hit next to home as I have walked in those shoes. I have documented that journey in my memoir, The Caregiver's Son, Outside the Window Looking In.

Sonny on a sunny Sunday is exactly what I personally needed. The man is a living testimonial to the power of God and believing in the Lord's healing powers. He told God that if he ended up being cured that he would spend the rest of his life serving Him with his gift of song. And he does just that, traveling around Horry County visiting churches and other venues. I say this was just what I needed because of news I had just received on Thursday. I had an appointment for routine lab work on Monday. I had been concerned yet again about my health. Never Google symptoms but I had done it again. I was convinced this time that I might have prostrate issues. Self diagnosis is not a good policy. A phone call from Doctor Lash Springs had good and not so good news. He reported that the results were good except for an extremely elevated sugar level, a reading of 264 pointing to potential diabetic ramifications. He asked for me to come in Friday before my annual physical and repeat the lab work. I had been praying for God to cure me and there was no indication that prostrate cancer was my problem. Still, diabetes is a scary premise. Sonny and his testimonial to God's healing powers uplifted me when I needed it most.

I realize that praying to the Lord does not always deliver the results we want but it took the worry away. I placed my fate in the Lord's hands. Tomorrow (Monday) at 9 AM I will face whatever life has in store for me. I have not lived my life as I should, but I cannot help but think that God has been patient with me because he has something else in store for me before I meet Him. But that is just my gut talking. Blame it on Cuz I reckon. He deserves the credit for pushing me into this pull. I am staying that course. This might just be symbolic, but Friday after I donated another batch of blood for testing, I bought my first ever gold-plated crucifix necklace. This was not planned. It just happened. And things like this do not just happen without reason.

Today has been a great day. After praying last night and again experiencing Sonny's story, I have had my best day in a long time. I feel I have received a blessing. My heart has been lifted and I no longer worry about my doctor's appointment tomorrow. I will take what is tossed my way and accept it. I believe in God's healing powers. Life is good. God is good. Right, Cuz?

Bonus round I say. We watched the second in a four-part History Channel series, Jesus His Life. This was about Mary and her impact on Jesus. I learned something in the first part about the Nativity. I never knew that the Lord's Prayer originated after John the Baptist being beheaded and was the prayer spoken by Jesus after finding out about his death. See, I am living and learning and moving forward. We also watched our weekly Sunday program, God Friended Me. It always leaves us teary eyed and inspired with its message.

Searching for purpose perhaps and I do not have all the answers for sure but just maybe by me writing about my journey into the pull and finding the Lord is what I have been called to do. By helping me, just possibly it can help others. No, I am not implying that what is happening to me is some great or special event other than how it has impacted my life. My fictional books often have unexpected twists that offer up those 'got you' moments. Me being pushed into the pull certainly tossed a twist in my direction, one I never saw coming. Most of my life has been wasted pushing back on the religious factor. As I have said many times, my reluctance has never had anything to do with me not believing in God. Every time I have been pushed toward it, I just always seemed to push back. I guess I still have no viable explanation for doing this. It certainly has not been from a lack of inspirational people around me. Granny Bowie is the perfect example of a Godly woman if there ever was one. As I have stated, my parents were never influential in me having a relationship with the Lord. They did not attend church regularly nor did they ever push it on me one way or the other. No, I am not blaming them. I take responsibility for my actions or lack thereof when it comes to church. I guess the timing was not right for me then, nearly sixty-four years in the making if you think about it. Judy has certainly prayed over the years that this would happen to me. A lot sooner than it eventually did. But it had to happen when it was supposed to happen. You are never too old I suppose. I remain on the path but doing it at my pace. I confess that I see the world around me and my personal world in a new light. I try to be more tolerant and forgiving than I used to be. I am evolving.

Sonny Clardy said it best. Try to seek out someone you have done wrong, had words with or a broken relationship with and reach out to them and ask forgiveness. I have given this considerable thought today. I have been practicing this with my Metglas golf buddies. Too often while working, before I retired, I would have little fallouts over what now seem like such trivial situations. Life is too short. Now I find myself offering counseling to members feuding over similar scenarios. I do my best to encourage my buddies to talk to those causing them grief. Long friendships should not be severed over golf misunderstandings. Sometimes they listen. Other times they are as pigheaded as I once was. I do my best to anchor the sidelines and not take sides. It puts me in awkward positions though when individuals decide they do not want to play with others and I still play with all of them. It is tough scheduling and inviting and working around foursomes without explaining why others are not playing when certain individuals are. It is not a fun place to be for sure. It is much easier when adults do not act like children. No need for me to toss the first stone as I have walked in those shoes before, as unpleasant and unrewarding as it is. Hey, I cannot solve their issues when I am still resolving my own. Mentoring is a tough row to hoe indeed. Life offers its fair share of lemons.

Forgiveness. I have dwelled on that today. I have pondered again what Sonny said. Reach out and ask forgiveness of someone I feel I have possibly done wrong or have said something I should take back. Interesting twist of fate has entered my brain and my heart; one I am not sure current people in my life would condone or

149

appreciate. I will have to pray on this and give it a bit more thought but, just for the record, I am going to toss it out there. I considered contacting my ex-wife. We were married for fifteen years and I severed that relationship for reasons I will not go into now. I have been happily married for twenty-four years at the time I wrote this, so why am I compelled to ask forgiveness now? Maybe we are all on the backside of life and it is easier to dwell on such subjects. To the ex, forgive me for perhaps not treating you with respect. There are two sides to every breakup. I should just take responsibility for my part. Again, this is in the thought process not the must do process right now. It would be easier to just let it go I reckon.

Still, Sonny's advice, ask for forgiveness haunts me. Is my choice the right one or should I seek another route? Grappling is not pretty. Digging up old bones can be worse. This would be an unprecedented step in my life. What to do, what to do? I think I might call my dear friend and brother, Tom Marsh and run it by him. He and I share a similar path, both of us in our third marriage. He is also a retired minister so who could be better to seek guidance from than him. I have wanted to call him anyway since he returned to West Virginia a few weeks ago.

I did not gain any resolution after talking with him. I even ran it by Judy and she basically told me to do what I was compelled to do. As it stands, I have not made that decision one way or the other. I have forgiven myself and I know God has forgiven me. Is it necessary for me to take it any further? Right now, I cannot answer that question. Maybe someday I will be able to come to terms with it.

The Envelope Please

Sometimes when you feel you are heading down one path, it forks on you and you are left standing there breathless and overwhelmed. Previous thoughts have been sidetracked and derailed. Forgiveness pursuit, not right now so it seems. I did mention that what we want is not what He delivers to us. He has a plan though. His might not be ours. I am not about questioning His. Doctor Lash Springs delivered the results of my second round of lab work. Good news: All my cholesterols, good and bad were good. Prostate was fine. Kidney and liver functions are working as they were supposed to. Blood pressure, pulse, temperature normal but that pesky blood sugar was still prevalent. It had dropped from 263 to 203, not that I understood these numbers. Drum roll…that placed me in the Type 2 diabetic category. Now what, I asked him? One pill a day to try to reduce it. He would also prescribe a gadget for me to use, testing my blood sugar every morning and after dinner. Track it for the next month with the goal to reduce the sugar level to 150. We would circle the wagons and meet to discuss the results in a month. He tossed another number at me. My A1C was 8.7, another number concept that meant absolutely nothing to me. My new goal was to get that number down to at least 7. He also recommended that I dramatically change my eating habits. Okay, I admit it. Not what I had hoped and prayed about, but I accepted the results and have not lost my newly found faith. Beats cancer doesn't it.

We pray for family and friends, especially when situations in their lives prompt us to do so. We pray for ourselves when we feel the need and focus. Just because we do not receive the response we hoped for doesn't mean the Lord wasn't listening. He always listens. He then delivers what He sees fit. Think of the alternatives. I could be dealing with something much worse. Diabetes is not the end of the world. It might not be where I would like to be at this time in my life, but I am still above dirt. There is a greater plan evolving. My gut tells me so. Look how Sonny's illness changed his life and has impacted so many lives since. I am still in that pull and somewhere along the way a powerful outcome will be the result. I will take this and my journey one day at a time. My spirits are high. My spiritual feelings are higher. Life is good. God is good.

I have high blood sugar, and Type 2 diabetes is not going to kill me. But I just must eat right, and exercise, and lose weight, and watch what I eat, and I will be fine for the rest of my life. Tom Hanks

Yep. The life change begins now. Will it be fun? Not hardly. Giving up or cutting back on the things I like to eat might have its challenges. My head is on right though. I can be quite regimented. I will do what I need to do. Unlike some diseases and illnesses at least this is controllable. So many are not. I seem to be healthy otherwise. Well, except for having two off and on bad knees due to ole Arthur. I had hoped to have gotten two more steroid injections but not optional until we get this high sugar thing under control. That is all right. God is with me and guiding me through the process. The pull has never been stronger. I am an active guy, and I am not obese. Diet changes, more exercise should take care of matters with the Lord as my Shepard.

When the doctor said I had diabetes, I conjured images of languishing on a chaise lounge nibbling chocolate. I have no idea why I thought this. Mary Tyler Moore

This was an appropriate quote. While thinking about cutting back on cookies and chips can be challenging, neither of these vices is what immediately concerned me. Obvious carb and sugar concerns for many are the urge to eat potatoes, pasta, and bread. I am not big on any of these. Fries are not a deal breaker for me either. Pasta, no big deal, and I rarely eat bread with meals. Well, for sure, it is difficult to eat a breadless sandwich or burger but being diabetic does not mean you have to go cold turkey. My alternative to Mary Tyler Moore's chocolate concern was cornbread and buttermilk. I often have my most favorite meal on earth three or four times weekly. Black skillet southern cornbread crumbled in a bowl with cut spring onions and then buttermilk added would probably be my last meal if granted one. It will be tough to come up with an alternative mixture for making cornbread. Fat free butter milk is available and is what we already use.

Confession time. Day 2 of my diet change I experimented with Pumpernickel bread which is the prime choice of all breads. I purchased a loaf as I shopped for my many food alternatives. I crumbled two slices of the dark bread into a bowl and added buttermilk. I must admit. It wasn't half bad. Seriously though, I will still work in my favorite dish; maybe not have it as often as usual. I will monitor the before and after sugar level results. Lord, please help me work through life's little pleasure. I joke about this, but I am truly thankful that I have Him on my side as I navigate the latest chapter in my life. I think back on Cuz. He had that rare leukemia with few options. His life ended way too soon. No. I am not questioning God's intentions in this outcome. I am just saying that what I am dealing with does not compare.

I think back to both my parents. Mama was diagnosed with pancreatic cancer and was gone in three short months. Daddy had Parkinson and Alzheimer's yet survived for many years, bedridden the last few. He eventually gave in three months after Mama earned her wings. Thank you, Lord, and the love I have for You will get me through this. Prayers do not always equate to cures. The outcomes can be more powerful than we could have ever imagined. I hang my hat on His plan and continued journey. I ask Your forgiveness for the mistakes I have made up until now. Thank you, Sonny. Asking forgiveness has taken on a clearer meaning. I was thinking too small. My eyes are open now. I see the big picture. My faith remains strong. Life is good. You are good, God.

Christ is the Good Physician. There is no disease He cannot heal; no sin He cannot remove; no trouble He cannot help. He is the Balm of Gilead, the Great Physician who has never yet failed to heal all the spiritual maladies of every soul that has come unto Him in faith and prayer. James H. Aughey

Tis the Season so it Seems

This is my second. My first was last year; my first to attend Maundy Thursday. It was quite different this time. Once the Word had been delivered, we lined up two by two in the main church aisle like animals entering the ark but only after we had removed our shoes. Instead of our pastors washing our feet, we would have our feet washed by the person ahead of us and then turn to wash the feet of the person behind us. Last year our feet were washed by the pastor and assistant pastor.

I had never heard of Maundy Thursday until last year. Shows you what a sheltered life I have lived. If it existed in the Pentecostal faith, I do not ever remember it being mentioned or ever witnessed anything close. Maundy Thursday is the Thursday before Easter and it serves to commemorate the Last Supper. Love one another as I have loved you, so commanded Jesus of his disciples. The pull is full of unexpected surprises.

Those first unique experiences continue for those open to accept and experience them I suppose. For the first time in my life, I am planning to up and at'um in the morning to attend sunrise service. The Atlantic Ocean will be the backdrop. Judy and various friends have attended sunrise many times. I usually just opted to rise at my usual time and attend the usual slotted Easter Services. I grew up like most with the attraction to Easter being dying and hiding eggs, receiving that Easter morning basket delivered by the illusive Easter Rabbit. That rabbit that nobody ever saw was the counterpart to Santa on Christmas. The rabbit would deliver a spectacular decorated basket loaded with candies and chocolates. Sometimes we even received dyed pet chickens and ducks. It is not every day you own a green chicken or a blue duck. I guess I did wonder why we did not receive pet rabbits instead.

Okay, so I am up before the break of dawn on a chilly morning. We are to gather at a designated beach front location not far from the church before the sun rises. The beach and ocean will be the backdrop for the service. Well, you cannot deny the ambience for the occasion. The first challenge upon arriving in close proximity of Plyler Park was where we were going to park our vehicle. We stopped at a restaurant a few blocks away. The manager was sweeping the sidewalk. I explained where we were headed and asked if he minded if we parked in his parking lot. We received a profound No, customers only. Not tossing racial stones but the Asian gentleman did not seem to appreciate the connection to Christ on Easter morning. We eventually located another spot and arrived a Pyler Park well before the service was to commence. Plenty of our church folks were there as well as an assortment of strangers. Our associate pastor would be performing the service.

During the service, two figures wearing hoodies passed behind the stage along the board walk in front of the ocean. They paid no attention to the singing or gathering. How can everything around them be important but not this I wonder? The sunrise rose with perfect timing over the ocean, a splendor to behold. Clear cloudless skies made for the perfect He Is Risen ceremony. We returned home after receiving our sunrise blessing and changed, readied ourselves for the regular morning church service, my first 'two for'. The pull remained in control of my journey and destiny, so it seemed.

The God Account

God certainly had opened an account on my behalf. He had been balancing the check books so far, ensuring my bestowed faith tokens were spent wisely. A little tongue in check certainly cannot be harmful. I have mentioned that we latched onto the new CBS Sunday night show a couple of years when it was introduced to the viewing audience. I cannot say that we were not concerned that the God Friended Me weekly serial might not be what we wanted to hang our hats on. So many shows of today make fun of religion. We decided to give it a try. Worse thing that could happen, we did not like it and would watch no more episodes.

For anyone who has never heard of it or watched it, the premise is simple. Miles Finer, the main character, is an outspoken atheist who has a pod cast where he spreads his disbeliefs. Already, we were concerned with the premise of the plot. This was sure to go south quickly. Miles journey begins when he receives these friend requests on his smart phone suggested by God. We are thinking sacrilegious comedy for sure, making fun of Christians. As it turns out, Miles and a couple of friends are tasked with locating this person from the friend request and ultimately assisting them in solving some crisis in their lives. Each episode thereafter becomes more complex and intertwined. The three captivated by the requests are obsessed with locating the perpetrator behind the God Account while still helping those from the request. Most episodes end with profound lessons and often tearful results for those of us watching.

Here we have an atheist who was brought up in a church pastored by his father. Yet, he is challenged with saving lives, solving people's problems while denying the existence of God. Miles is convinced God is not behind the account. It must be somebody human. My take, God picks the unlikely to serve his purpose and spread the gospel. Miles is caught in the pull. He is not willing to accept it or believe in it. His atheism is constantly challenged but he sticks to his guns and denial. I am not sure where the writers intend to eventually take us, but I am hoping Miles sees the proverbial light eventually. There is hope for everyone. Look at me. No, I was never an atheist, nowhere close, but the light appeared because of Cuz dying. In Miles case, he turned the other way after his mother's death. Because God did not save her, he does not believe there is a God.

I am not sure what sent my friend, Little Goober Head, down this path but the birth of his daughter and the death of Sammy did penetrate his unbelieving ways apparently. I can only pray that he continues to drift into the light and finds the pull as I have. He is a lot younger. Look how long it took me. One thing for sure, belief in God or prayers to God does not always end as we think they should end. Let's face it, we do not always get our way in any given circumstance, God or not. I do not think entitlement is part of His plan for us. Contrary to this, the younger generation is being groomed to think they are special, entitled to everything and have no accountability, no responsibilities. I want it now, not later, so seems to be their mantra. A rude awakening is ahead if they do not wake up and turn to the only one that can save them. Sorry, you are owed nothing in life. You are born and you will someday die. It is left to you how you spend that in between time. It is no more complicated than that. Sure, I did not see it this way when I was young either.

There are few shows on television or in the theaters that are feel good family viewing, ones with a message and a belief that keeps you on track. My opinion, Blue Bloods is one of the better ones. Sure, it has its share of violence, but it adds in just the right amount of family interacting in each episode. There is always a scene featuring the family around the dining room table and blessings are recited. And then the issues of the day are discussed. They each strive to be the best they can and hope to do the right thing in the end.

Too many series on television are intent on passing their values onto us, tempting us to accept the new normalcy in life. Same goes for almost every commercial on TV. The family is skewed in directions to sublimely cause us to accept it. Movies are no different. I hold no ill will toward anyone's lifestyle, beliefs, or the way they wish to live their lives. It is theirs to do, theirs to bear. I do not appreciate their values being force fed on me. Flaunting it is not necessary. I get it. Push me. I push back. If you are my friend you will still be my friend no matter what, unless you resort to force feeding me. Even then, hopefully we can have a friendly discussion and agree to disagree and set a new tone going forward.

I am certainly not one to critique and criticize anyone. I have ventured down my fair share of poor chosen paths for most of my life. I have no right to judge anybody. I have chosen the new me and will continue to follow the pull. I will share what I have learned in my journey if you are interested in hearing it. I will not force it on you. I already know how it feels to be on that side of the fence and I fought back as well. Life is short. God is Good. I will venture where the pull draws me. Eventually I will get there.

Irrelevance

The world as we know it has gone completely wacky in recent weeks. It is March 2020. A mysterious virus has brought life as we know it to a screeching and grinding halt. All was well, better than well and now that has all changed with the invasive virus than originated in China, Coronavirus, Covid 19. Everything that we have grown to depend on is no more. All sports have ceased. All colleges and schools have closed. There is no such thing as the dine in experience. As mandated by the government, only take out or drive thru is allowed at any restaurants. Theme parks, national parks, campgrounds, playgrounds, all social gathering are in shut down mode. Name it and it is temporarily no more. Only big box stores, grocery stores, pharmacies and medical facilities remain open to the public. Most shopping is gone except online. People are encouraged to stay home, work from home if possible and gather in crowds no larger than ten.

It is critical to protect the elderly because they are the most vulnerable. The elderly or those with medical issues can die from this virus. Yep, we fall into that category unfortunately. Even the churches have closed their doors in an attempt to protect and preserve the flock, much of the congregation falling into that at risk category. The younger crowd is being asked to please follow the recommendations even though the severity of the virus does not threaten them nearly as badly. It is critical that they comply. If not, they can be carriers and infect those of us doing our best to take all the precautions. We are in this together, us and the rest of the world while the scientific community attempts to come to grips with the nature of the beast, a way to contain it, treat it and hopefully eventually come up with a cure and vaccine.

Life is not comfortable for any of us, those trying to exercise a self-imposed quarantine and house confined lock down with exception of the necessities like groceries, medical supplies, and doctor care. And we are only early into week two of this world changing experience. Society is on the verge of collapse and the only thing that can save us is staring at us in the mirror. This only works if we pull together and make it work. So far, hope is alive. I cannot say this has been easy, especially if you watch any news on television. Gloom, doom, and a chaotic world will cause doubt in the strongest. I have been one of those wallowing in doubt lately. We have watched the bottom fall out of the stock market. A blissful life of retirement has never been scarier, watching life's savings evaporate by the minute. It certainly does not help, the major news programs showing us the ticking time bomb on the television screen as the market plummets. Hoarding has reached epic stages. Of the craziest, people emptying the shelves of toilet paper and paper towels. I don't get it. Sanitizers are virtually gone as well but there is something terribly wrong with society when you witness people pushing shopping carts with a zillion rolls of toilet paper piled head high.

Yep, uncertainty and nervousness have set in. I catch myself thinking what is next, rioting, fighting, rationing, curfews, or maybe even martial law. Judy tells me she is not worried and puts her faith in God that everything will be all right. No denying it, my faith is a bit rattled and is being tested. I guess I am slipping back into a safe place for me, my usual normal, pushing a bit against the pull. I am losing confidence in mankind to prevail as everything that once was routine has now evaporated and vanished quite quickly.

Society has never faced such harsh adversity on all levels before. The media feeds our fear. Too many of the politicians rub their greedy little hands, thinking they have us exactly where they want us, at their mercy and dependent on them and them alone. A president and his cast of virus and economy fighters are updating us daily on where we stand and what they are doing about it. Nope, there are no sports worldwide, but a scorecard is being posted, winners and losers highlighted and a ticking clock warning us that time could be running out. I have allowed myself to be sucked into this vortex, falling somewhat back into my old ways of viewing things. I am not in the hoarder stages yet and I have not gone over the panic-stricken cliff, but doubts are creeping into my thinking and my heart, so it seems. I am a human reacting as too many humans are reacting, losing scope of where I have come up until now.

Sometimes we just deserve a stern slap in the face or swift kick to our backside to make us focus, take a breath, close our eyes, and squash the paranoia. If no one delivers the reassessment blow then maybe it can be delivered differently. That brings me to my morning devotion, March 19th from Men of the Bible. Today's devotion was titled Irrelevance, The Ten Spies. At first glance, the title meant absolutely nothing to me which is not uncommon in my journey into the pull. Ten spies were sent out from the Israelite camp to check the land for a possible new beginning. These men came back spewing negative information saying while it would make a wonderful home, it was the home of terrible giants that made the men feel like mere grasshoppers by comparison. Moses had really sent out twelve, not ten. Joshua and Caleb spun a more positive perspective and encouraged the people to venture into the land and take possession of it. Most were paralyzed by the challenge to possess the Promised Land.

The lesson, faith is a major element in our relationship with God. God always keeps His word. There were ten examples of crippling doubt and two examples of enabling faith. Question, which one will you follow as you face your giants? When you focus on God and his ability to overcome obstacles no giant or barrier will appear too large or too strong. It does not mean that there won't be battles to be fought. The key is entering the fight with the sword of God's Word and the shield of faith to ensure victory in the battle. And just like that, my fears, my worries, my concerns had been quenched and my faith had been restored. God would protect us from the giants of adversity out there if we were willing to have faith in him and carry the sword, He had graciously given us.

I no longer allowed myself to become caught in the fear mongering wave being painted by the news media, the naysayer politicians, or the nonbelievers of society. I then became aware of all the feel-good stories out there, a nation pulling together, a world tossing the best that could be had at this invisible foe with but one goal in mind, to lick this as soon as possible and restore and save the world from ourselves. Some have insinuated and even referred to scripture that this is God's plan, to restore order to a chaotic world and make us appreciate Him, family and not be caught up in the modern-day conveniences, perks and luxuries that have spoiled us and have skewed our perception. Maybe it is His way to slap us in the face, kick us in the butt and a chance for us to understand what is most important, Him, family and having and living the faith.

When will this mess end? I cannot say. Will we come out of it for the better? We can only hope and believe and hold on to the faith. No doubt, we have a long way to go yet to make believers out of everyone, especially the politicians who think we should worship and depend on them instead of God. Satan has his pawns as well. The battle, good versus evil has never been more critical than it is right now. To find our Promised Land though, we must first slay the proverbial giants. To do so we must stick firm to our faith and love of God for this to end successfully. The pull still has many tricks up His sleeves, so it seems. Takes one to know one and I am back on track.

Streaming, Not Screaming in Challenging Times

Sunday, March 20th, the battle against a deadly and unknown virus continues. All church activities have been canceled, including all church services. The rule and advisement prevail. Stay away from congregations of people and this includes the congregations in the simplest sense, church. So many might question, if it is God's plan to restore faith and love of God, how can this make sense by now not having church. Others say church is merely symbolic and a conduit for worship. Prayer can be practiced anywhere. It does not require that we gather inside a building to worship and have faith in the Lord. Still, some struggle to stay true to their belief and their faith if they do not have the man behind the pulpit to steer them down the straight and narrow and to deliver a message that they might not receive otherwise. That alone speaks volumes, oh ye of little faith in the first place.

First Church, the church in the heart of Myrtle Beach, the church with a heart, is not the only church worldwide facing something no one saw coming, no organized church services. Take a breath before you go off the deep end and think the devil now has us where he wants us. For years church services have been televised. Any given Sunday, on a wealth of channels and networks, you can find pastors, preachers, and evangelist addressing their flocks. Yeah, but some might say, these are not my preachers, my reverends, my pastors, or my places of worship. You are not getting it if you think this way. God is not simply your church. Having faith, loving, and believing in Him do not just exist inside of manmade structures. Okay, we must first get past this and it is where we take a deep breath and reconnect to our faith.

Let us, just for the sake of argument, say you are really struggling latching onto a televised church or evangelism leader. Modern technology has arrived. We at First Church were already a leg up on this pandemic. Our Sunday services are televised on a week delay on a local Fox network station. Each week's service is recorded and replayed the following Sunday. And to further the cause, our church had already begun streaming the service live on Facebook on our site, @ FUMCMB. With the technology already in place, and with a little tweaking, our church ventured into a new concept. Sunday, March 20th, the service was made available live at 8:30 and again at 11 AM, the normal times for our church service.

I merely hooked up the laptop to the big screen television, logged into FB and then clicked on the FUMCMB site and we were in business sitting from the comforts of our sunroom at 8:30, our normal time for attending. No congregation, no problem. Pastor George, Assistant Pastor Meredith, our choir director, Norman, our pianist, Scott and our Anew church director, Grant, were present to deliver the message of God. Yep, this was another first, sitting in the sunroom for our church service. Now we had watched the delayed version on an occasional Sunday when we had missed the live version. See, faith and love of God, prayer and worship know no boundaries and are not confined to just inside a church building.

Amazingly so, I shared the link to our service on FB for anyone interested, saw an endless supply of posts from friends and strangers who had been watching their churches or others doing the same thing, streaming live, or recorded on FB. God and the Word is all powerful. Just maybe God's plan all along was to make us realize this fact and to bring family together in an entirely new format, one in the comfort of their homes at a time when we needed it the most. I realize that everyone can put their spin on it just as they can spin what is happening right now. I prefer to build on something positive and avoid the negative rhetoric spewing on television. The blame game, we should have done this, shouldn't have done that, should have said, shouldn't have said rhetoric is of little interest to me. Reading something into what someone said or did not say solves nothing. Using tragic circumstances for monetary gain or to empower those who already feel they are the almighty powerful is pathetically wrong on every level. In the end, there is only One that matters. I pity those that do not get it and try to rule by deceitfulness and corruption. You know how this played out for others who lived by that mantra. The pull is alive and well.

First Church stepped up its game for those of us in house confinement. Now they are providing a live FB devotion at 8 AM daily with Jennifer titled 'Morning Joy', 'A Moment with The Ministers is at 11 AM with Pastors George and Meredith and 'Julia's Story Time' at 1 PM for the children. Reaching people has never been easier. Stir craziness is preventable with the appropriately prescribed medicine and dosages. God remains Good.

Not Journaling is a Journey Just the Same

I was quite persistent and diligent when I first began journaling. It was my intent to make this a daily occurrence. I managed to do it for awhile and then discovered that my life did not always allow for daily entries. This is not exactly the truth. There is really no excuse. I allow time for all the other pleasures or necessities. It's like prayer or like daily devotion. If you allow it to be part of your life it will be just that. I pray every night before I go to sleep. I read my devotion every morning; well, most mornings. Maybe I do not journal everyday but that does not mean that I am not learning or having lessons tossed my way. I just do not document all of them. Living it is the important aspect of life. So, I will try to catch up a bit in this summary so to speak.

Judy had elective surgery recently on her right foot. This altered our life as normal long before the collapse of society arrived with this China virus mess. After surgery she had to wear this large and cumbersome bandaging on her foot and leg. In addition, she could not walk and had to use a knee scooter. The bandage was removed after a couple of weeks but was replaced by a hard cast which she ended up wearing for several more weeks; no walking and still using that scooter. I became somewhat of the caregiver during this time. I am not complaining. On the contrary, I embraced my new responsibilities. It was more difficult for Judy, not one to like being waited on or be able to do the most common tasks. After about six weeks, the cast finally came off and was replaced with a removable boot. The scooter was replaced by a walker. We adapted and life continued.

We had begun getting her out a little, even when she was still in a cast and using the scooter. She weaned off the walker and we were getting her to church finally. As for me, I attended church throughout this time she could not, a first for me. There was a time when I would have used her excuse as an excuse for me to stay home. Not this time. I did not miss a Sunday while she viewed the delayed telecast each Sunday on Fox. With me as her chauffer, I ensured she was taken anywhere she wished to go, including out to

166

eat, church, church activities, brief shopping, etc. And then the restrictions and closings related to the virus hit, a mere two weeks until her next doctor's appointment. Try to put yourself in her one shoe. Now church, church activities and dinning out was taken out of the equation after she had already endured ten weeks of altered states and semi-confinement. Still, throughout, she held firmly to her faith even when stir craziness nipped at her heels.

In a week we find what the doctor says, boot, no boot, more walking, driving? The day before her visit, the two-week mandated virus rules will be evaluated and then a decision will be made to extend them, restore them, or restrict them or whatever. Next week will be interesting from all fronts, hers personally and ours collectively. Sometimes journaling is not fun, especially with uncertainty hanging over you. Keeping the faith on all fronts, we will live with the consequences tossed our way. That is just what we have learned to do, putting all of it in His capable and loving hands.

Watch for What you Wish

I have stated many times how dreams play an intricate part in my life and how I often use them for writing material. Then there are those Cuz related ones that I so look forward to, but rarely occur now. Speaking of Cuz, with the craziness and uncertainty of today and the wacky world of virus mania, I had this sudden urge to see him. No, not Him, but Sammy. I am not turning my back on God, nor am I asking for Sammy to intervene by any means. I just miss Sammy and it has been forever since I have dreamed about him. Maybe stupid, but after my normal nightly prayer, I reached out to Sammy to pay me a well needed visit. Hindsight, was this an appropriate thing to even consider or do? Could it be interpreted as me circumventing God by reaching out to Sammy? I meant no disrespect to our Savior by taking a perceived back door approach to one of his heavenly beings. Ultimately God decides what we need, not us, but what is done is done.

A dream quite vividly entered my nocturnal escape. It was not Sammy though. Instead, I received a six for one swap. And as always, I latched onto the dream and pressed the record and rewind buttons throughout the night to ensure I did not forget a single detail. Here goes. I found myself in my first house located on Dundas Road in Abbeville, South Carolina. I was not alone. My parents were there, as well as my grandparents, Papa and Granny Bowie. A third couple was present in my home, Granny's sister, Aunt Nelly and her husband, Uncle Compton. Oh yeah, like Cuz, these six are deceased; long ago deceased for some. No Sammy but boy did I have my hands full.

Mama and Daddy were insisting that I take a vacation with Granny and Papa to their favorite getaway, the Smokey Mountains. My grandparents loved going there, spending a week in the little efficiency cottages along a stream. I had vacationed with them once as a kid with Aunt Nelly and Uncle Compton along, something they did often. I was pushing back, imagine that. I did not feel the need to go on this vacation and voiced my opinion thusly. I suggested that my parents should go, that they probably needed it worse than me.

Aunt Nelly and Uncle Compton remained neutral, no speaking parts for them apparently in this dream production.

Eventually my parents informed me that nobody was going then. The next thing I remember is that a long folding table had been set up filled with an assortment of food. Mama told me if I wasn't going to agree to go then they would stay there with me. I then tossed my hands in the air and ventured down the hallway. Before reaching the bedroom, I heard strange noises emitting from the darkened room, something scary and not of this world. I cautiously approached and then peeked inside. There I saw a monstrosity on my bed beckoning for me to come to it. No way. I resisted and returned to the kitchen alone. Standing there, I peeked out on the carport and spotted someone curled in a fetal position on a makeshift bed. I could not see this person's face. I needed coffee but could find no cups or mugs in any of the kitchen cabinets.

I then woke. It was 3 AM. I was lying on my right side with my right arm curled underneath the pillow, one of my typical sleeping positions. Something was different though. My arm from shoulder to hand was ice cold. This was not mere numbness like when your arm, leg or foot goes to sleep when you accidentally cut off the circulation. My arm was not asleep. It was not numb or prickly. I moved it easily. It was freezing cold though, exactly how I would imagine a cadaver's arm feeling. I was on my back and placed my arm by my side. It was cold still, obvious when I touched it against the warmth of my side. I tucked it underneath my body to try to warm it. The covers were up to my neck. That is it. That is all I remember. When I got up at my normal time, I did what I always do, I checked my blood sugar as instructed by my doctor. It was 151. It had been averaging 119 for months and had not been in the 150s in the morning in nearly eleven months. I have read that the key to a low morning sugar is a good night's sleep. Mine had been restless. The next morning it checked 111.

So, what is my takeaway from this odd dream? I am not an expert on dreams for sure. I had ended my prayers asking for Sammy, not God's interaction. Had that been my mistake? What if Satan interpreted this as a sign of weakness and he had influenced my dream instead. Significant people were placed in my dream, loved ones. They had offered to help me but could not. Maybe this was meant to be false hope. Then there was that demonic creature in my bedroom taunting me to join it. After that, the stranger was on the makeshift bed just outside my door. Could that figure have been God, close by and seeking me to come outside and check on Him? Did I fail or pass the test then? I refused to leave my house even when tempted by people I knew and loved. I then refused to enter my bedroom and join something purely evil. But, ultimately, I failed to check on the stranger in need camping out on my carport.

What did my cold arm have to do with it? Could that represent a piece of me almost yanked from the pull because I put my faith in wanting to see Cuz instead of God? I had gone around God to try to see Sammy. Maybe that is the lesson learned. Ask for Him and do not bypass protocol for selfish reasons. Watch what I wish for, dreams and remembering them vividly. God is Good and the pull continues to control the outcome.

All Things are not Beachy

People have their dream vacations and their favorite destinations. These might range from the mountains to the sea, a beach getaway often a preference among many. I grew up with my parents venturing to Daytona Beach, Florida, if not every year, at least every other year. My dad loved racing. Two weeks around July 4th were a given to partake of the big race there. Even long before I would qualify for a driver's license, I knew my way around Daytona as well as I did back home in Abbeville. Family did family things in my time. The big one, the annual vacation, was a given. We would go some place during the summer for at least one or two weeks. As I have stated I am fortunate that I saw much of this county growing up. My folks may have been a tad short on faith, but they always put family first. I recap this only in preparing for this segment to frame a beach destination in the Palmetto State, Myrtle Beach specifically.

Up until the mid 90s I could probably count on one hand how many times I had ever vacationed at Myrtle Beach. For lack of any explanations, we just did not go there very often. As an adult I never gravitated to Myrtle Beach either. The mountains tended to tug at me more and it is not because I do not love the beach. I do. I guess as a married adult, at least during my first two marriages, we did not often take the big one. Rarely did we go on that weeklong vacation and never on a two week stay. Not sure, maybe times were harder. Vacations seemed so expensive when the expense was not being covered by parents. Looking back, this is about the best explanation I can manage. I can only recall one time with each of my first two marriages that we did venture to Daytona for a vacation. I don't ever recall going anywhere in either for a week though. That is twenty years collectively. One thing for sure, my heart was not aimed at faith and family was not the top priority apparently. Two divorces prove that point I suppose. All fairness, there are two sides to every split up. I am not excavating buried bones though. The past is the past, and I will leave it there for now.

In 2004 I lost my dad and my mom. Mom was diagnosed with stage four pancreatic cancer just days after Christmas 2003. We had spent

Christmas with them before heading to our Windy Hill Beach condo for eleven days. Obviously, the phone call of her being in the hospital sent us packing and back home. Given the dire situation we sold our house and moved in to take care of my parents and grandmother. I have recanted how Mom died three months later. Daddy died three months after her to aspiration as we fed him his pureed Sunday dinner. Tough losses for an only child.

I interviewed and received a job offer in Conway, just a stone toss from Myrtle Beach. I moved to our Windy Hill condo and began work Jan 14, 2005. I commuted back to Abbeville every Friday after work and returned on Sundays to begin my work week on Monday. Six weeks later were secured a home at the beach and relocated Granny with us. She had never lived anywhere except in the Abbeville area. Let me say again for the record, I had never considered ever working or living at Myrtle Beach. Judy's daughter, son-in-law and grandboys lived in Conway so the decision was not difficult. Before then though, I could have listed my top twenty places to live and Myrtle Beach would not have made that list.

Most people move or retire to the beach because it is their choice, something maybe they have always dreamed of doing. It did grow on me after we purchased our beach condo a few years prior. Beach life is supposed to be relaxing, tranquil, sea, sun, and sand in your shoes. My physical prior to starting work indicated I had high blood pressure. That is not supposed to happen when you move to the beach. I have donated blood all my life and never have there been any signs of high blood pressure. So much for a relaxing beach life. Looking back now, maybe it had been brought on by the stress of being a caregiver and then losing both parents. Welcome to the beach and blood pressure medicine.

Six weeks after the move, Granny's health, which had been declining, worsened. Ninety-four and outliving your only child cannot be the easiest thing to endure. She gave in and joined Papa, Mama and Daddy, leaving me as an only with my entire bloodline gone in an eleven-month span. I struggled through a depressed stint for a while, self-diagnosed of course. We visited Abbeville one weekend shortly after Granny's death. While there we received a phone call and the number appearing on Judy's phone was our home number at the beach. The policeman was standing in our kitchen reporting to us that our house had been broken into at the beach. Among the stolen items was a shotgun that Papa had passed on to me. The thieves even stole our Spam. Welcome to the beach.

Still our first year at the beach, I noticed a festered bump on my knee. Like most men, I poked and picked at it until it burst. Over the next few weeks, it would not heal, and the knee reddened and felt hot. I visited the doctor and she prescribed antibiotic medication. This was early December 2005. Over the next few weeks, it was not getting any better, my condition wasn't either, loss of appetite and feverish. My doctor sent me to a specialist and culture samples were drawn. A day or so later I left on my lunch break to review the results with the physician. The hospital was less than five minutes from work. The physician would not let me return to work and had scheduled me for emergency surgery. I phoned Judy. We were keeping both grandboys for a couple of days. She arrived just before they took me into surgery. I had a serious staph infection and remained on an IV and in the hospital for a week. I was released just prior to Christmas. I did not know it at the time, but I could have died from this. I had to wear one of those healing pumps affixed to my knee for a couple of months. Welcome to the beach.

Oh yeah, our Murrells Inlet home was on a golf course adjacent to a par three green. We had no privacy, and I was struggling getting accustomed to living on a postage stamp lot. I was accustomed to having a large vegetable garden and this situation and losing my parents was not sitting well with my disposition. After five years we moved to Pawleys Island. We had a large yard, an even larger house and swimming pool. It was about this time that Judy retired a second time, no longer doing mortgage lending from home. I had a forty-minute commute to work in Conway in the morning and sometimes an hour home in the afternoons. She was not happy living so far away from everything in Pawleys so eventually we sold and moved a third time. We ended up more centrally located in Myrtle Beach. Three moves in about ten years, welcome to the beach.

In 2015 I decided to retire. The timing just felt right. We had witnessed how my parents had not had time to enjoy life before illnesses took their toll. I did not want this to be me. I did continue to work part time over the next three years at Metglas where I had retired. I could have continued working part time, but again, it just felt like the right thing for me to do. Now I had plenty of time to write, play golf and enjoy family. Welcome to the beach finally. Funny thing though, when you live at the beach, many of us hardly ever go to the beach. I cannot explain this. We were less than ten minutes from the ocean, yet we rarely ever saw it except on Sundays from church near where the old Pavilion once stood. It is worth mentioning, I never set foot in the Pavilion Amusement Park but once. Duncan, the older grandboy was four when we took him there for his birthday. That was before we moved to the beach, Welcome to the beach just the same.

There is always calm before the storm or storms in this case. Hurricane Matthew approached the Carolina coast in 2016. It had quickly strengthened to Category 5 status. It hugged the eastern coast and eventually arrived in Myrtle Beach as a Category 1 with 75 mph winds. Zone A along the beach was ordered to leave. We were in Zone B, between Bypass 17 and Business 17. We were not ordered to evacuate so we stayed. The storm passed with the front side a little scary but not what you expect from a hurricane. The backside hit with vengeance dropping trees everywhere. We saw trees fall in the street in front of our house and in yards and the street behind us. We did not receive any damage but were without power for several days. I have never seen so many downed trees and destruction. We learned our lesson. We would not sit out another. Welcome to the beast. I mean the beach.

One year later, say hello to Hurricane Florence. Remember this story already told. Florence's landfall destination kept everyone on pins and needles up until the last possible opportunity for potential evacuation. When the orders were finally given, it was given to all three zones, A, B and C along the coast. I experienced the power of prayer and the delivery of the prayer all so powerful. More hurricanes. Welcome to the beach.

Now, in 2020, we face possibly our largest challenge, not one for just Horry County, nor South Carolina, but of the United States and the world. An invisible enemy has brought the world, our great nation to a screeching halt. Coronavirus is wreaking havoc, taking lives, and crushing a once prosperous economy. I pray now harder than I ever have. Some blame God for this; not me. Some say this is God's way of showing us what is important, and it isn't sports, movies, social media or even work. I am not saying I buy into this. Others think the Devil is pitting his power and forces against mankind, evil challenging good. Some are even questioning where God is and why He is allowing it to happen. Not me. We are learning that we can indeed live without sports and all the social aspects in our lives. Real families are becoming families again. Those that are not, just don't get it yet. Some never will.

The city of Myrtle Beach has decreed that all entertainment venues must shut down. Many golf courses are closed. Tourists are being asked to leave by a mandated date and hotels are being told to not take any reservations until May. The governor has warned any new arrivals to the state must self quarantine for two weeks. A once thriving beach community has taken a hit worse than in a landfall hurricane. This storm is bigger than all of us. One thing is constant for one who is still firmly caught in the tow of the pull. I pray. I pray a lot for us, for the United States, for the world. I pray God will work the miracle only He can. I pray He will destroy this virus and allow a world to heal. I think others like me have come to realize the power and love of the Lord. God moves at His own pace and His desired way. Possibly He is sitting back to see how we handle this adversity and how many finally turn to Him. Possibly this is a lesson learned by all of us. Believe and trust in God and everything will be fine. Welcome to the beach. Welcome to the world. God continues to be Good under any circumstances.

Gas and Go

We are just days away from this two-week Coronavirus social distancing deadline. Our president and his task force will assess where we are in this vicious battle against our invisible enemy. We have diligently practiced social distancing. We continue to utilize the power of prayer and profess our love for Him. We wait as does the nation. Is there light at the end of this darkening tunnel? How long can this great nation survive in virtual shutdown? Becoming antsy and experiencing stir craziness is only natural. We have done our part, staying home except for grocery runs. Realistically, there is really nothing we can do. Most everything is closed including stores for shopping. There is no dining out; only drive thru, takeouts or delivery. Grocery stores, Wal-Marts and pharmacies are open. We keep the faith and believe.

Everyone reaches their tipping point though. We decide we should take advantage of the low gas prices and venture out to refuel. And we decide that while out we should support the local venues by ordering takeout. At Costco we find no lines at the gas pump. Gas is an incredible $1.45 per gallon. I cannot recall the last time gas was this cheap. We are packing though. We have Clorox wipes, sanitizers, and rubber gloves for our little family outing. We resemble a duo heading out to perform emergency surgery instead of the mission we are on. Those at other pumps offer mental relief as they too have wipes and gloves.

With a full tank of gas and from the safe confines of our vehicle, we ride our normal route of shopping in abnormal times. None of the stores that we would normally shop are open. We skirt by them, window shopping the shielded walls not offering a peek inside. We venture many blocks up Kings Highway surveying the territory, those venues open and offering food pickup. On 60th Avenue we u-turn and retrace our route, finally settling on a restaurant to support local in these troubling times. We pick Big Mike's Soul Food, a local mom and pop favorite. Parking in their lot, we dial them up and place our order.

After they deliver the order curbside to our vehicle we return home from our adventurous trek and say grace before enjoying the home cooked meal. Tomorrow we will repeat our outdoors adventure by refueling the second car and supporting locally. We joke that maybe we should offer this service to our neighborhood. Allow us to take your car, refuel it and bring you takeout, our way of escaping boredom, us giving back so to speak. It is so ironic that something as simplistic as gassing up the car feels like a social event. Dressing up and heading out was quite satisfying even if we remained inside the car for the most part.

We have no idea what lies ahead for any of us and just how this virus will take its toll. We have no control over the outcome. I continue to pray that God will take care of us and do what He has planned for us. I did pray that it ends sooner than later but that is my wish, maybe not His plan. We continue to watch our church's daily devotions and messages on Facebook. God remains a strong and constant factor in our lives. Like my own, I have no idea where this journey may end. I can only pray and put my faith in the loving hands of the One who does know. Welcome to my life at the beach and in the force of the pull. God is Greater than ever in a time that we need Him the most.

Socially Distant

March 28th, I continue somewhat of a routine in times that are the furthest from resembling routine. I read my devotion each morning seeking inspiration and guidance. We watch Jennifer on Facebook as she delivers her devotion for First Church, our church. Pastors George and Meredith continue to have their moment with the ministers on our church website as well. We even watch the children's segment. You cannot get enough of spiritual influence, that's for sure.

My today's devotion was titled Courage to Cry Out, the story about Bartimaeus, the blind beggar. He took advantage of Jesus being in town and kept yelling to be noticed so that Jesus would cure his blindness. He did this despite the grief he was catching from everyone else. Lesson, never allow etiquette to stand in the way of crying out for Jesus to meet your special needs. It might annoy others, but faith never annoys Jesus. Keeping the faith in times like this, a virus bringing us to our knees is the perfect time to cry out to Jesus to save us from the hardships and terrible consequences.

While we are expected to practice social distancing with others to keep this dreaded disease from spreading, we don't want to distance ourselves from the Lord. If ever we needed Him to hear our cries it is now. Death and destruction in the world is happening before our eyes as sure as plagues ravished Biblical times. Prayer does sooth the soul and it fends off the need to worry over things you cannot control. I remain upbeat and positive, keeping the faith that everything will eventually be all right and better than it ever has been. Thinking and believing otherwise is not giving God the credit He deserves. Yes, lessons are being taught and hopefully learned amidst the crisis, something that will make each of us stronger and closer to our Creator.

On a lighter note, and not belittling the crisis we face physically and spiritually, we ventured out on the second road trip. Road trip might be a bit overstated, but we ventured outside the confines of our home and neighborhood again. Call it another family outing. This time we chose a different route, northward on Business 17, onto Ocean Boulevard pass the state park. It was sad passing empty hotel parking lots in wonderfully sunny and warm conditions. Typically, only the threat of a hurricane could have transformed the beachfront into a ghost town. With hurricanes though, once they are gone, clean up and recovery is in full throttle. With this Covid 19 threat there is no timetable for normalcy returning along the Grand Strand, our country, or the world.

We motored up the boulevard, just past the Sea Captain's House. Eventually we turned around and backtracked until arriving at Magnolia's, a favorite beach eatery. This time there was no buffet open for business. Home cooking was being served by takeout only. We decided to support local once again and it did not get any more local than supporting a restaurant owned and operated by one of our church family. After retrieving our home cooked meal with all the fixings, we drove over to Costco to top off our second car one buck forty-five a gallon. Getting gas was the closest thing we had to a family outing and social activity right now, dressing up with at least some place to go.

Yep. these are indeed strange times. Spring day, perfect weather, retired and living at the beach, yet society has crumbled because of an invisible foe threatening the world as we know it. I am so glad that I have a relationship with God now. If I didn't, it's no telling what I would be thinking and doing. Keeping the faith and loving family are powerful tools in times of need. The toilet paper apocalypse continues, insanity reaching new heights for those set on hoarding their priceless tissues. Sorry, I still do not get it but one thing for sure, those responsible are making it tough on the rest of us. Scooping up every bottle of sanitizer and wipes are selfish acts. Don't they get it? This only works if everyone has an ample supply of sanitizer and wipes. Logic has been lost in the land of the lost. Lord, see us through this and only You can. For now, we will continue practicing social distancing from everyone but You. My faith remains strong that the world You created will survive and we will be better once this is over. The Sabbath comes tomorrow and with it we will celebrate it with You as we always do. Feeling the pull stronger than ever…

Side note: Roman Reigns, the wrestler that has battled leukemia, decided to bow out of WWE's WrestleMania. The WWE planned to stage the event in front of an empty arena and then later televise on PPV. Reigns did not want to jeopardize his health, even if his disease was in remission. All other sports and entertainment have stopped but greedy moguls of the wrestling industry persist in keeping the show going when the show is no longer important in the big scheme of things. Go figure.

The New Normal

This is the second Sunday of the country's virus shut down and we sit in the comfort of our sunroom viewing our church's service, one absent of a congregation. The new normal has us congregating at home in front of our computers, iPads, smart phones, and televisions to worship the Lord in a virtual reality world. This has become the new normal, our laptop attached to the big screen smart television viewing the modified message from its Facebook post. Even though it feels odd sitting on the couch in my shorts and with a cup of coffee, what isn't odd is staying strong in our faith that God will make the world whole again. The music and message are uplifting. We embrace our abnormal Sunday morning, one spent spiritually with our church family. It is what it is, and we adapt.

Pastors George and Meredith tag out as they deliver the sermon, each adding their personal experiences that fit into the morning message. The scripture is of Lazarus rising from the tomb. Pastor George adds his personal story, a throwback to when he was a high school basketball point guard. George smiles, short of stature, saying he did not fit the image of a basketball player. He admitted he was a poor shooter but could dribble and pass the ball around. His team is leading the game by two points with mere seconds remaining. They have the ball. Strategy is clear. The opposing team will foul the weakest shooter. George takes the pass expecting to be fouled. Instead, they part and allow him to go down court with less than ten seconds on the clock. Their strategy was to allow him to shoot and then get the ball back. George finds himself wide open in the lane and is faced with two options. Shoot the ball and make a shot he clearly makes 99% of the time or hold the ball and allow time to expire. What does he do? He shoots the ball and misses. The rebound by the opposing team is tossed down court where a player tosses up the ball from half court, nothing but net at the buzzer. Game tied. There would be overtime thanks to George. George said his team played an excellent overtime winning the game. He had the best view from the bench.

At graduation, his coach signed his yearbook saying if given the choice to score in life, don't make the shot, George. Even with the outcome his coach had obviously referenced, George disagreed with the advice. When facing adversity and uncertainty, you have no opportunity to win if you do not take the shot and give yourself a chance to win. Powerful message indeed! My morning devotional reading was titled Peer Pressure. The essence of the message after reading the scripture was simple. Standing up to peer pressure never feels comfortable, but when you refuse to yield to ungodly pressures, you greatly encourage and bless those who look up to you as an example of faithfulness.

Facing the invisible evil as we are doing now, I interpret this for me as sticking to our guns and following what the professionals tell us to do. Practice social distancing. Wash our hands and sanitize as best we can. Oh yeah, remember how I was opposed to using hand sanitizers. Toss that out the window. I use them almost obsessively now, even carry a small bottle in my pocket when we do venture out. I have not played golf in a couple of weeks even though some of my playing partners have tried to encourage me to do so. Being of the elderly persuasion, we fall into that at risk category. I also have type 2 diabetes putting me at a greater risk. Yes, we have ventured outside the confines of our home briefly occasionally, but we practice sound judgment and exercise the recommended precautions. As tough as it might be to remain home, we have remained strong. Myrtle Beach has made it easier for us by closing most of the venues that might otherwise have tempted us.

Giving in to peer pressure or making poor decisions is not a viable option where your health and safety is concerned. While making the shot is important in any victory, choosing that shot to ensure victory is more important in what might be an exceptionally long season. The pull guides my decisions. So far, I have not given into temptations. We stand strong, stay home, and hunker down, forever embracing God, our faith and believing all will be well in due time. Time, we have plenty of, as far as we know. Then again, our time on this earth is not our choice. We will take the shot when we control the game. Right now though, we will rely on our Godly coach to call the plays and guide us to victory.

Forced Family Fun

My devotion this morning was scripture referring to how Jesus honored and treated the women in his life. He respected them, unlike how most men treated women in Biblical times. In times like these, social distancing, people unable to work, schools and colleges closed, churches closed and no dine in restaurants, with few stores open for shopping, challenges to family have never been tested more. There are no outlets for children with most malls closed, no theaters, parks, or bowling alleys open. There are no sports to watch, poof, gone and recreation sports gone as well, make or break time for many family households.

The President just announced an extension of the two-week country shut down, now saying this new normal would continue through April. Fast forward. It is June 30th, a long way to go with challenges only going to worsen for most. Families have two choices; adapt and learn to live civilly under one roof or drive each other crazy. Hopefully, new family values will be discovered with families bonding like they never have before and putting God and faith back in play. We are but two under the same roof, no kids, no pets, unless you count my aquarium fish. We have found that we can make this work, love never more alive in a world where home confinement is constant. Respecting one another, respecting each others space while still enjoying each other has been a piece of cake in the big picture.

Today we plan our third road trip in four days. We are excited with the premise of leaving the house and the neighborhood. No, we are not taking great risks and, as before, we'll have our survival kit along, sanitizers and gloves. Today we will venture to Socastee Hardware to refill the gas grill tank and then to Costco to fill my five-gallon tank used for lawn equipment; good time with $1.45 gallon gas. These would have normally been my chores. Today though, it is a family outing, just leaving the house if only to do the simplest of tasks. We will again choose takeout to support locally.

When I was pushed into the pull, I knew there would be challenges. I figured most would be all about me, my journey and learning where

I needed to go. I could never have imagined that in a time when I was being pulled the country would virtually come to a screeching stop while battling such adversity. People dying everywhere was not what I thought I was signing up for, not that it changes where I am heading. It does impact the trip though, but in a good way if this makes any sense. No, people being sick, dying or losing their jobs is not a good thing; far from it. My point, it has only strengthened my faith. Without a first-time relationship with God, where would I find myself in such a crisis?

I am at peace right now. I could have been panic stricken, stressed and angry if the old me was in charge. Stir craziness might have taken its toll. My disposition would probably not have been admirable. I am none of these things. My mood is more laid back than it ever has been, even without playing golf now in several weeks. Life revolves around faith and family, just that simple. How long will I remain in the pull is anyone's guess. As Pastor Buddy told me, there is no timetable, no right or wrong way to get there. Maybe there is no actual ending to the pull. Being forever pulled in the right direction possibly is a lifetime journey. I do not have those answers yet. I will just continue to follow where it pulls me.

My prayers have been simple lately if one can call prayers simple. I stopped focusing on individuals in my life, family, friends, us. I have shifted my prayers to this country, to the world and God protecting all of us and doing what He has planned to protect and save us. It is not my place to question why this is happening and what end is in store. I am human though. It hurts to see so many suffering and dying from this virus. Hopefully, mankind, families are turning to their Creator, no matter what religion they practice. More importantly, they are asking forgiveness and showing their unconditional love to the only one who has the cure. Crazy as it sounds, this was not my usual approach to something as grave as these times. That was then. This is now. FFF, forced family fun might be the plan. You must spank your children sometimes to show them just how much you love them. It is our time to pick that switch from the bush and to be taught to change our sinful ways. God is Good and only He knows what is best for His children. Tough lessons often require tougher love. I get it. I just hope everyone else does.

Ironically, last night I dreamed I was in this crazy scenario where I was saving people from a monster, an evil that was transforming people into ugly distorted beings. Best I can describe the dream is that it was a cross between the movies The Blob and The Thing. This Blob Thing would fly airborne and cover its victims, eventually combining the victims as one multiple person mass, the people aware but unable to move or act as one in their newly formed deformed body. It was my job to bring them to safety while trying to destroy the creature responsible. Did I win? Did we succeed? I do not know. Maybe I should interpret it as the battle continues, many sequels remain, good versus evil never ends. The enemy can take any shape, any form. God gives us the tools to identify and destroy it if we believe and if we listen. Coronavirus is our new enemy. We will win this one if we trust in Him. Love conquers all in His kingdom, the world He created for us.

Noah Knows Best

My morning devotion was about Solomon preparing to take over the leadership from his father, King David. He could have asked God for riches and fame but instead he asked for wisdom. God granted his wish and made him wealthy and powerful to boot. We continue to be challenged by this virus attacking the world that God created. We could ask Him for plenty in these scary changing times, even material things like the illusive toilet paper but are creature comforts really what this is all about it. Sure, those without jobs are suffering. Children are no longer in school. The thumb screws continue to tighten, our president, federal and local government asking us to do more each passing day to minimize the risk of spreading this and possibly killing unfathomable numbers of people. It is natural for people to become angry, fed up, bored and bit stir crazy if they are doing what has been asked.

Facebook is flooded with this comment and that, warnings, and opinions. Some continue saying this is the devil's doing. Others still believe it is God's will for this to happen. Neither blame nor credit holds much merit. If Satan is behind it then enough said. If God has His hand in it, He has a purpose, a method to the madness. Questioning either serves no purpose in the big scheme. Believing in God and His love for us is critical. Practicing what we preach is a must, a given and the only obvious solution.

It hit me this morning out of the blue, maybe my revelation of things to come. I am not a prophet. I am no saint. I am not even a visionary. I am just a common everyday ordinary old man caught in the pull of something special. This is my take, right, wrong, or just my two cents worth. What if this is something of Biblical proportions? I am not forecasting an end of the world scenario. I would never do that except in my fiction writing. I am leaning toward the lesson learned from Noah and that ark, something indeed of Biblical proportions. Could the virus be our flood? It started out as two weeks of self implemented social distancing and now by presidential decree has been expanded much longer. That forty-day time frame comes to mind. Our homes are our safest places to weather the storm, our personal arks.

We are all sinners, even the most religious of us. Humanity in general has distanced itself from God and church. Christians around the world are persecuted for believing in God. Social media does not like people to mention God, church, or the Bible. Worshipping sports, sports figures, movies, movie stars, material things are more comforting to humanity. Having money, power and social status is more important than being thankful for what we have. Families are no longer families. Blame for this used to be placed on broken homes and marriages, parents not being parents, everyone being the center of their universe. The family unit is indeed broken. Smart phones, social media and the 'it's all about me' factor have created a form of social distancing to the family unit long before this virus arrived.

Strip from us sports, movies, school, gathering places like malls and parks. Close everything but what is considered essential to our survival. Force families to become families again within the family household, the family ark. This scenario will be a make-or-break situation. The family will again become a unit for those realizing the importance and significance of what is happening, our forty something days confined to the ark. There will be losses. It is inevitable. The strong will survive and will be stronger. You cannot remove God from every aspect of our lives and remain happy or think that God is going to sit idle and watch it happen. Tough lessons we are going through right. Possibly we had reached our tipping point in His eyes if He is indeed responsible. Only He knows.

In Biblical times as well as throughout time, He chose the right people to do his bidding. Most of the time, He does not necessarily choose the most religious from the flock. He picks the most unlikely, the naysayer or one that has what it takes to carry and deliver His message loud and clear. Some say that man is Donald Trump, our president. Our president is rough around the edges, does and says a lot of things we do not like or appreciate. There is no denying it though that he loves this country. He quit his plush life to be our leader. He donates his salary to worthy causes and works on our behalf freely. He does not play politics and gets things done. This terrifies those who have been in office forever and have treated us as mindless sheep. He believes in religious freedom, God, and the Bible and has done more than any other leader of this country to emphasize their importance. Those most iconic figures in the Bible were persecuted, attacked, and often put to death for doing the very same thing.

Maybe God has chosen him to be that person, one that cannot be impacted, manipulated, or influenced by those who do not believe or think they are more powerful than God. Just maybe Donald Trump is our Noah, one who can guide us through this storm and ensure we are better and stronger. Just yesterday at one of the president's daily virus task force briefings, if you call these marathons brief, he allowed a few of the CEOs to speak and explain what their company was doing to support the cause and fight this invisible enemy. Industries had refocused their energy to produce more needed product than they ever had or had completely shifted their manufacturing capabilities to provide the country and world with the critical components to fight this war.

Each laid out a compelling commitment. Then Mike Lindell, the founder and maker of My Pillow products stepped up to the podium. He is one of the few owners that can say his product has never been produced in China or any other county. His products are made in America by Americans. He had converted a large percentage of his manufacturing capabilities to making face masks just like other CEOs had promoted in their turns ahead of him at the podium. His predecessors had thanked the president, the vice president and task force leaders for what they had been doing. Mike did the same. He ended his time with an unscripted add-on, saying that people did not read their Bibles like they should in times like these.

The media went berserk, literally crucifying him for doing this. How dare he bring Bibles and God into this? This just verifies the concept of Christian persecution. Take God out of school, out of the government and belittle churches or anyone publicly speaking such rhetoric. We are in the middle of critical times, an opportunity to pivot to what means most. Plenty of us are embracing God and believing in Him. Everyone must decide, pick their side, and hopefully choose the life ring being tossed our way. Continue to be hateful toward your fellow man and continue to threaten those trying to help and somewhere down the line you will reap what you sow. Picking the side of God is the only one that will guarantee victory. Finding God when I did has never loomed larger than it does now. No brainer for me, stick with our modern-day Noah and ark, eventually we will sail out of the turbulent storm. Obviously, many may not get this until it is possibly too late, just like those begging to board the ark after the rains began. It will get worse before it gets better. I am prepared for the journey and will ride out this storm on the winning side, His. Pull on…pull on.

After this entry, I saw the following posted on social media. It was uncanny after having recorded my thoughts.

The flood lasted 40 days.
For 40 years Moses fled Egypt.
For 40 days Moses stayed on the hill to get the boards.
Exodus lasted 40 years.
Jesus fasted 40 days.
There are 40 days between Carnival and Easter.
40 days tell the woman to rest after birth.

So, what about the Bible and the number 40?

A group of theologians think the number 40 represents 'change', it is a time of preparing a person or people to make a fundamental change, something will happen after these 40 days.

During quarantine, rivers are clearing up, vegetation is growing, the air is cleaner because of less pollution, less theft, less murders, the Earth is at rest for the first time in many years.

In the Bible, whenever the number 40 appears there is a 'change'. During that time, enjoy it and return to the family altar together. It will be a great blessing, and you will see the changes that God can work in you and in your home. You will see that 'everything works together for good for those who love God.' Romans 8:28.

Remembering that we are in the year 2020 (20+20=40)
40 days for the spiritual liberation of our nation, the best is yet to come.

Well, this was an interesting and profound post if ever there was one. The next day I read another spin on this Coronavirus. Someone had written a segment asking us to think about what was happening. The virus was much more dangerous for the elderly, those possessing the knowledge and wisdom to see the truth. The old folks could not be tricked by Satan because they (we) have gone around the block a time or two. The elders could see through the deception being tossed out by the Devil and would forever believe in prayer and God. Satan's plan is to eliminate those who are best equipped to fight him and train the younger ones for the battle ahead. Get rid of the wise ones with this virus and the younger variety would be easy pickings. Eliminate the church goers and bible toters first and the remaining flock can be brought to slaughter. Scary thought, but conceivable given today's war against Christianity and the fact so many of the younger folks are drifting away from God and church. The devil feeds off the angry and hateful, those thinking they are entitled to everything. Offer up free and the weakest will take the bait and follow. Temptation!

These are two takes on what is happening, a virus with us in its grips. I prefer to trust in the first scenario, something wonderful will be the outcome. I have never seen so many posts about scripture, praying and God before. People are stumbling over themselves trying to help their fellow man. Families are becoming families again. The world will indeed be a better place once we weather this threatening and all too scary storm. Believe, trust, and pray. I have certainly come a long way to be thinking in these terms. And no, I was not 40 years in the making.

PSD

Each day brings more change in this world of virus control. I never imagined that my personal journey would be impacted by something of such epic proportions. I figured this would just be my journey, not the journey of the world. Mine has become something of unimaginable scope. The state of South Carolina, one of the last states holding out, has now mandated a stay-at-home order. Hunkering down will reach a new untested level. We continue to be in the grasp of PSD. **P**racticing **S**ocial **D**istancing is not for the wimpy, weak, or unwilling. You are either all in or you are not. Wiggle room is just as bad as not doing it at all. It is for the protection of the elderly and a means to flatten the curve they keep telling us. People are indeed dying from this pandemic. This is of Biblical epic proportions for sure, a world being brought to its knees. On ones' knees has never been better justified. Taking a knee to pray is not a sign of protest or showboating. Life has humbled us.

Golf, something I did twice weekly is not that important. One of my golf buddies just sent me a text and asked me to play golf with him and a couple of my ex-coworkers. I declined. I explained that we had been trying to do what was asked of us PSD wise and I was not willing to mess that up for a game of golf. He said he would keep a spot open for me at the designated tee time on Friday, two days from now. The next day I received another text from him. He and the others had decided to follow my lead and had canceled the round. Leading by example beings a positive influence for my pals was quite gratifying. Each of them is in my age bracket and each has medical issues that put them at a greater risk. Life is more important than golf. There will be time for enjoying the links once this has passed.

Judy has been a seamstress seamlessly making us masks since you cannot find them anywhere. Like toilet paper, hand sanitizer and Clorox wipes, they have vanished off the face of the earth. She has done quite well improvising, one from a bath cloth, another from her panties and two others from Coastal Carolina scarves. With no golf, we are walking and biking in the neighborhood, all the while keeping our distance from anyone during our route. She even made a recent comment that lately we are talking more and communicating better, a family of two growing closer while confined. Our love and faith have never been stronger.

My scripture this morning was from Genesis 45:7-8. God has an amazing way of using even the worst circumstances for our good. To Joseph - God has sent me ahead to keep you and your family alive and preserve many survivors.

In difficult times it is important how you respond. So far, we are stress free even with the uncertainty of today and many tomorrows to come. Faith, family and forever grateful, we take the virus situation in stride. The light at the end of the tunnel is shining brighter than ever. We remain thankful everyday for what we have, each other and the spiritual confidence that the best is yet to come. So many others are seeing the light as well, some probably for the first time as they too have been caught in the pull. God remains Good.

A Direct Line

Dreamland invades my world once again. I tend to cling to dreams that in my humble opinion hold some significance. In this one, there was something evil and lurking in the woods. I was with two other men. I have no memory of their identities. We were in the woods and something menacing was after us. We were looking over our shoulders, moving from tree to tree and were doing our best to stay hidden from whatever was stalking us. The other two suddenly bolted, apparently willing to toss caution to the wind to outrun it. I chose to remain hidden, my back against a huge hardwood tree. I risked a peek, but I did not see anything.

After some time, I suppose convincing myself that whatever it was had chased them, I made a hasty escape as well. Next dream scene, I was at my parent's home on Marshall Avenue in Abbeville. Inside I tiptoed down the hallway of their ranch style house. At the end and to the left was my Granny Bowie's room. This is the room she occupied after selling her house to move in with my folks. Granny's health was exceptionally good, and she was in bed. I eased alongside her bed and just sat there, confident that I would be safe long as I remained in the room with her.

I knew in real life what a Godly woman she had always been. I often joked that she had the Red Phone, a direct line to God when she needed him. She woke and smiled; glad I was there. We began having a normal conversation, nothing that involved evil monsters. She encouraged me to make a bedside pallet on the floor and stay in her room. No argument from me, I felt completely safe and at ease in her presence, a woman who had passed fifteen years ago. Mama opened the bedroom door and saw me there on the floor. She told me it was my turn to stay with Granny and she then barked out my marching orders, what would be required of me. I told her no problem and then the dream segment with my granny ended.

Next, I am on the back pew inside the Pentecostal Church in Abbeville. The preacher is calling people to the alter. In the dream though, I heeded the call and walked to the alter. I don't remember what happened when I got there. A few minutes later we were dismissed, only to be called to come there again. Fewer people came each time, many having left the church. After a third time I was the last person standing in my pew. Nothing scary happened that I can remember. I decided it was time to leave the church and Pastor George, our pastor in Myrtle Beach, walked with me to the door and into the parking lot. He told me he knew what a Godly woman my granny was and to be with her as much as possible. I told him I went to her home on South Main Street for Sunday dinner. We did this in real life when I was growing up. This is the last thing I recall.

Now comes my spin of dissecting the dream. I interpret it like this. Maybe, through the dream and using someone as saintly as Granny, it was God's way to guide me through potentially evil times. There is this monster virus out there attempting to scare and threaten us, to control every aspect of our lives. Like the monster in the woods that was after us, we never saw it but knew it was there. Lesson, if ever my faith is shaken and tested, turn to those in my life that are Godly, strong in faith, and devoted to the creator. Granny would fit the bill. Trust God and trust those whom God put in our lives. Even though Granny has been long gone, her presence and love still embraces me. God gave her a kitchen pass and sent her to reassure me that all will continue to simply be fine if I hold the faith and succumb to the pull. As always, this is just one man's interpretation of a dream, the furthest from an expert in the field. She might have subbed for Cuz.

On a non dream point, I completed my next doctor's appointment. My A1C was 6.3, slightly up from three months ago when it was 5.8. He was pleased with it. He told me to continue doing what I was doing, and he would see me again in six months. This spoke volumes to me because stress, mental and physical, can impact blood sugar levels. Keeping the faith and being at peace with God's hands on the steering wheel, I am not stressed out by this abnormal lifestyle we are living with this virus threatening us. I have remained calm, at peace and totally confident that everything will be fine. A couple of years ago this might have been a different story. I thank you Cuz for doing your part in my journey. It came at a great sacrifice though, losing you to cancer. As we are less than four days away from Easter Sunday, I must remember how another man sacrificed himself for us.

194

Something tells me that this Easter will be the greatest one ever. The world is taking note and again believing what some have long forgotten or have never experienced until now.

He Is Risen, Virtually So

2020, fourth Sunday of not attending church and instead we are still watching it on Facebook via the large screen television. This week we have continued our virtual vigilance, watching the daily devotion, Moments with our Ministers Monday through Saturday. Last year we attended Ash Wednesday, Maundy Thursday, and Easter services at First Church in the heart of Myrtle Beach. We had even attended sunrise service at the beach this time last year. Today though, due to the confinement caused by the virus and the directives delivered by our government, we stay true to our PSD chosen path. Four weeks in, it is tough to be on an island, two faithful souls marooned and loving each other and forever believing in the Almighty.

It is troubling though, even in a time of undeniable faith, that there are those still attempting their best to stifle Christianity even as Christians learn to adapt. Work arounds to the faith and our Father continue to amaze those like me new to this. While restaurants, pharmacies, grocery stores and most creative venues have evolved to pick up and drive-thru, so have many of the churches. Some pastors are offering drive-thru confessions, the clergy sitting in chairs in parking lots as the flock passes through, stopping long enough for a quick prayer, blessings, or confession opportunities. Other more creative preachers have gone to a throwback technique, utilizing the outdoor drive-in concept; cars parked in rows as if viewing a movie on the big screen, while the preacher delivers the message from an elevated stage and sound system. A church is not just four walls as some believe. Its lifeline is the people, no matter where they are. Streaming has never been utilized more than now as the ministers deliver their message on Facebook, You Tube or via television networks. God's Word is being delivered or taken out, your choice.

Still, the Devil and his devious disciples work ferociously to deny these ever-evolving mechanisms to keep God alive in a world denied them because of this virus. I for one, like many others, find it difficult to follow local, state, and federal government methods through their madness. It is perfectly acceptable for Wal-Mart,

Target, Home Depot, Lowes, and liquor stores to remain open for business while other stores, parks, beaches, lake boat ramps, hair salons and sit-down restaurants are forbidden to operate. Even strip joints are being given a pass in many places. There is nothing more the opposite of practicing social distancing than going to any of these so-called essential businesses, fighting for toilet paper and sanitizer. Luckily so far, our experiences have been uplifting when we have had to venture into the world of this invisible enemy.

Now, the unthinkable and unexplainable has happened. The war on Christianity has stooped to new deplorable and despicable levels. Some local governments have forbidden churches from having drive-thru or drive-in services. A town in Mississippi brought in their police force during an Easter drive-in service to ticket those participating in their vehicles, ordering them to go home. Everyone in each vehicle was given a $500 fine. To add insult to this, the officers, not wearing masks or gloves, ordered the drivers to lower their windows, handed them the ticket and a pen to sign it. They were concerned about these people attending not practicing social distancing while inside their vehicles. Yet what did they do. They made them roll down their windows ticketed them. Satan is alive and well and using his army to break up our new normal of worshiping the Lord. The joke is on him, we cannot be broken so easily.

While we did not do any drive bys, drive-thrus, and drive ups, we did watch our church service virtually. The magnificent seven led us through the Easter service. I say seven because only seven were present celebrating it in an otherwise empty church. After watching our service, we watched two hours of Fox's special on the faith of America. It began with Franklin Graham and Michael Smith in New York's Central Park with the hospital tents as the backdrop. Then Fox took us around the world, talking with various clergymen and viewing the many unique ways that America was worshipping virtually. God is alive and well, stronger and better than ever and never has the world's faith been so focused and thankful for Him. Devil, you may as well go on back to Georgia and let that fiddle player whip you again. You are a lost cause in our lives. United, we are the church outside the walls built for worship. Franklin Graham said it well, 'With God in our boat we will not sink even in the worst storm.' Pulling me yet further, all I needed was that encouraged Cuz push.

Eyes Wide Open

The morning devotion got me to thinking in week five of confinement as the world battles this evil, invisible foe. It was from Psalm 88:1-2 with the scripture, *O Lord, God of my salvation, I cry out to you by day. I come to you at night. Now hear my prayer; listen to my cry.* In summary, the lesson states that the times will come when you wonder where God is gone during such suffering. You might even catch yourself wondering if He hears your prayers. Be confident though, even if He remains silent, He still loves you.

It is easy in tough times to feel like the Lord is not listening just because He has not answered your prayers. I pray every night lately for His love and wisdom for us to end this madness, but I have not lost the faith, nor do I feel He is not listening. There is a method to this madness even if I do not yet understand it. Suffering and death are facts of life. To be honest, we are extremely fortunate. We have not suffered like those that have been ill, many who have lost loved ones and friends or have lost their jobs because of this massive shut down to our country. We are doing well considering.

My eyes are open wider and more alert than they have ever been. I notice things that I normally would have ignored. God entering my life has opened my heart as well. I pay attention to the signs and the injustices tossed at Christians and their faith, and love for God. I find myself less angry and more understanding. I am more patient now. I know everything will be all right eventually.

I guess what troubles me though is all the anti-God rhetoric. It is interesting how now my awareness of this has been elevated due to my newfound relationship. I somewhat compare my evolution to that of politics. No. I am in no way saying politics and religion are on the same playing field. What I am saying though is that my world was similar when I paid no attention to politics. Like my journey into the pull, my path into the world of politics was a long one as well.

I do not recall politics ever being discussed or debated in our household. Maybe I just paid no attention. I have no recollection of my parents being a democrat or republican or somewhere in between. Growing up I did not watch the news, nor did I ever vote locally, statewide or in any national elections. I was not interested, just that simple. Regardless of the nominated party I did not complain or critique it. I had no dog in the hunt because I did not vote. One politician was the same as the next from my perspective if I even had a perspective back then. I never voted at all until 1991 and then only because Judy wanted me to vote for George Bush. At age 38 I voted and then began paying attention a little to elections and politics. Boy, looking back, I wish I never had. Likening this to my relationship with God that took me nearly sixty-five years to open my eyes and heart. Unlike voting and politics, I do not regret this decision.

That brings me back to my awareness level. I now pay way too much attention to politics and the corruptive craziness of officials elected to support us but instead utilize it to support themselves and pad their pockets. I also pay attention to what the various so-called leaders are saying and doing. Politics has somewhat ruined my disposition and faith in those who are supposed to be working for us. I still live by the creed of limiting discussions of politics and religion in a work environment or when among family and friends that think and believe differently. Strange though, government restricts the mere mention of God in schools, on government property and other venues and those same hypocrites will not hesitate to throw God and religion under the bus every chance they can. Some examples come to mind.

Franklin Graham was asked to use his humanitarian organization to build and establish tent hospital facilities in New York's Central Park to assist in the fight against this dreaded virus. Without hesitation he did. Ironically, there are those in the gay community that are bashing him simply because he and his followers believe only in marriage of a man and woman. Asked about this he basically said that the premise was true and that his organization's hiring practices required that anyone who worked for them support this biblically. He further clarified that neither church nor hospital turned away anyone in the gay community, no discrimination against race, color, or political affiliation.

Governor Cuomo recently commented on the issue of his state showing signs of flattening the curve against the coronavirus pandemic. He was quick to then exclude God in his governmental address. In his words, "The number is down because *we* brought the number down. God did not do that. Faith did not do that. Destiny did not do that. Lot of pain and suffering did that." Odd, isn't religion and God supposed to be excluded from any discussion and awareness from a government perspective. God only comes into play when He can be blamed or discredited for political gains.

Possibly the most troubling asinine statement came from the all-knowing senator, AOC. She is about anti America and anti God as they come. If ever anyone disputed this or supported her actions, I think the following extinguishes the argument. These are her words concerning the virus.

> *I hear many people saying that President Trump embodies the virtue and morality of Jesus Christ. You know, I must agree. Trump and Jesus are a lot alike. They are both con artists who duped millions into believing their BS. Look at Trump. His followers are a cult. They blindly believe everything he says and think he is flawless. It's pathetic.*

> *Two thousand years ago, a man named Jesus did exactly the same thing. He convinced his own cult that he was the son of God, of all things. How ridiculous is that? How can you be the son of something that does not exist? It's hilarious! Trump's followers are generally God believers as well. They are the easiest to manipulate. After all people who believe in talking snakes and talking bushes and magical daddies in the sky who can do and know everything are obviously not the brightest people. Jesus was a grifter. Trump is the same. Only idiots follow either of them.*

Yep, getting involved in the political arena was possibly my worst mistake because I now pay attention to what the politicians are doing and saying, or maybe more appropriately what they are not doing for us and those that are speaking disrespectfully of anyone that disagrees with their agenda. Venturing into a relationship with God has opened my eyes to the evil in this world, much of it centered in politics. Evil always tries to destroy good or to distort and discredit those who believe in God and hold firm to their faith. The war on Christianity has been around forever and has never been more persistent as it is today. Keeping one's eyes open as well as one's heart will defeat any enemy out to destroy a world created by the Lord who loves everyone, even those who dare to strike him down. Wow, did I just travel down this path? The pull is all powerful. Keeping the faith in our Lord is the most powerful tool of all though.

Just a Simple Prayer

God, thank you for another wonderful day in the world You created for us. Forgive us for our sins and trespasses. Thank you for what You have done for us in this time when we are doing our part, practicing social distancing in a world crisis of epic proportions. Please continue to protect our family and friends. Please protect those that are still filled with hate and do not believe in You or Your love for them. They probably need You more than many of the rest of us in this time of uncertainty. My hope is that they find a way to be shoved toward the pull if it is their time to do so. I am humbled by my relationship with You and continue to do what I can to show You my faith and love for You. Thank you for what your son did, sacrificing himself for us. In Christ's name, amen.

I don't pray out aloud, but I do pray within and do it every night after I crawl into bed. I am often criticized that I do not pray outwardly in church as much as I should or that I don't sing. Trust me, you would not want to hear me sing. I am told I don't smile or laugh enough. My response: I smile, laugh, sing, and pray on the inside. It is just my nature to be mostly unemotional outwardly but very emotionally internally. To that, I can become quite tearful in touching moments or movies that tug at the heartstrings. I look at it this way. There is no right or wrong way to display emotion, like the pull thing and no specific timeframe dictated. Simply said, my way is just my way and it does not necessarily have to mimic yours or anyone else's. We are all different. Different can be just as good as following the herd. I have always embraced being different, not that being different was my choice. Sometimes life just steers us down different roadways and at different speeds. The route might be shorter or longer but eventually we arrive, some of us later than others.

I Believe, Even When

Yes. Our church did reopen many months later, but it was not church as we remembered but open just the same. First Church had transformed because of the Covid concerns. There was no choir, only the choir director and a handful of masked and socially distanced church employees. The congregation entered and exited through only one door. Sanitizer was staged at the entrance. Ushers led individuals, couples, or families to the pews. Every other pew was taped off to keep everyone socially distanced. The pews were marked off in three sections, the ends, and the middle. Tape marked the spots down the center aisle to ensure proper distance was maintained. Everyone was required to wear a mask and the masks were to be worn for the entire service. There were no collection plates passed around. There were no hymn books or any literature in the pews. There were no handouts as you entered to indicate the order of worship. Everything you needed to do was projected on the walls on both sides of the church like a theater screen production. But we were back live, in church and we returned the first day the doors were opened.

The crowd was small. Those feeling uncomfortable or those with preexisting conditions were encouraged to remain at home and watch the service online. There were no hugs, no congregating about until after the service ended. The ushers signaled the departure, back pews first until all were empty, each social distancing. Outside we could visit in the church yard while still practicing what was preached, socially aware and respecting one another's space. We were the lucky ones though. Many churches were still closed in the area and across the nation. A Baptist church nearby was holding church services in their parking lot. Yes, we were blessed. This new protocol remained in place throughout the remainder of 2020 with no relief from those determining our fate because of the virus.

A few months prior to Christmas one of the church officials, Jennifer, contacted me and asked if I would contribute to the church's Advent. I said yes even before I understood what was being asked. Explained, I was being asked to submit a devotional themed

'I Believe, Even When.' What a year 2020 had been! Isaiah 40:09 implores us to "Raise your voice and shout, raise it: don't be afraid!" This verse prompted the Advent devotional book.

I eventually found the right time to sit in front of my laptop and compose my submission to the Advent book. As had become the theme, my heart took charge and compelled my fingers to key my thoughts effortlessly. I did it in one take, no editing, no rewriting. I submitted what I conveyed as a rough draft to Jennifer via email. She said it was wonderful adding she appreciated me sharing my story. That submission was used and appeared with twenty-six others for daily devotions dated November 29 through December 25. Mine titled Defining Moments was published for the December 3rd devotion. I had not included a title on the draft I had submitted so I do not know if Jennifer or someone else came up with the title. I never asked.

Sad to admit but I did not understand the concept of the Advent devotional at the time and even after it was printed for church members. Call me naïve or stupid. My dear wife explained the premise to a dumbfounded newbie. I have decided to include it below.

Defining Moments

To believe you must first become a believer. I have always been a believer that God is real, no denying that fact. I lived my life on the right side of most wrongs thinking there were always far worse sins to commit than those that I probably had. God is supposed to forgive us for our actions, right? Not that I ever gave it much thought while living my life my way.

For nearly 65 years I stumbled and fumbled my way through life justifying my actions or maybe not. Defining moments can often take a mere believer to another level. I lost my cousin to leukemia. Two years older than me, Cuz was my best friend, more like a brother I never had. Losing him impacted me more than any loss I have ever faced. It was then that merely believing did not seem to be nearly enough.

Struggling with these feelings I met with our pastor and did my best to explain them. He looked across his desk and told me that the death of my cousin had pushed me into the pull. That pull was me developing a relationship with God, 65 years in the making. He added that there was no right or wrong way to heed to the pull and no timeframe to get there. Just believe in God and follow where He led me. My cousin believed God is good. Caught in the pull, I believed in His love, His guidance, and His forgiveness. I believe in prayer because the bible tells us so. You cannot mock, denounce Him or those who believe in His greatness. In these troubling times, there is no greater time to believe.

Take time and listen to country singer John Rich's new song 'Earth to God' as it puts what is happening in perspective. The first verse goes like this:

> Earth to God. Come in, God.
> I know you're there, hearing our prayers wherever you are.
> We need you now, to send your love down.
> Take away the pain in your holy name. We ask this now.

The second verse:

> We're holding on, but not for long.
> Can you pull us all close to the holy ghost and keep us strong?

Powerful words!

Believe in the Almighty and the power of prayer. The pull is a wonderful tug to follow, your way, your timeframe-just heed to that push when you feel it. Believing is seeing the light knowing that the brightness of Him will set you free. Amen!

Winged, What a Feeling

Losing friends is not easy. It seems this year has been a tough one. And ironically those friends that I have lost were not causalities of Covid 19. In a time when Covid deaths are tracked like some awful scoreboard nightmare it is almost refreshing to hear when someone did not die from this dreadful disease. No, I am not celebrating non Covid deaths or deaths in general or trying to sound morbid; far from it. Plenty of conspiracy theories exist, questioning if every death dubbed as related to Covid is really fact or fiction. My celebration of life will forgo that argument and stick with the loss of those who meant so much to me and how my world was rattled when I heard of their passing. Unlike when Sammy died, I am in a better place spiritually now.

I have never dwelt on death and I guess I still don't, but I do view it differently. I suppose when God is nearby you find comfort in it. I have always said there is no need for me to worry about something I cannot control. Once your time comes you cannot change it and your time will eventually come up. That is a given. I have probably hedged my bet more times than I dare count with my reckless behavior, and I am far from being a cat with nine lives. Our church has lost more members or family members this year than some churches have members in their congregation. Sadly, given the events of this coronavirus most funerals were delayed for what seemed like forever. So sad for loved ones and friends being robbed their closure and chance to celebrate the life of a loved one.

I struggle to understand the premise behind rioters and looters being able to congregate in large numbers, but churches are prohibited to have funerals and weddings. Hordes can roam the aisles of large stores while Christians are robbed of their God given rights. It is tough to remain on the sidelines but the losses of those I loved had nothing to do with the travesties plaguing the world. I often must pray that God reels me in for thinking ill thoughts and viewing these situations so distastefully. That old red skinned devil always does his best to distort our thinking and corrupt our hearts.

Our most tragic losses are often the Lord's best gains I suppose. Those making it to his kingdom are, in an odd but profound way, the lucky ones. I lost three people that each played quite unique roles in my life and at oddly enough, in different times in my life. No, Sammy is excluded from this trio. He stands alone, however, at the top of the heap as my greatest loss, not that my parents and grandparents are to be slighted. With Sammy it was simply different.

John Speed Hall, Speedy as we called him, was a dear friend. Most have stories of growing up with a childhood friend, one who they had been friends with since they were old enough to know what friendship really meant. Speedy is not that friend. We were not diaper buddies. We met when we were high school. He and I attended different schools the first through sixth grades and lived on opposite sides of Abbeville. I met him after the various grammar schools in the county merged into one high school as seventh graders. Even then we were not instant friends. To be honest I am not even sure how we first became acquainted and later became friends. It just happened.

Mary and Ed, his parents became my second parents and their home, my second as well. His brothers and one sister became my kin, an only child with a huge, expanded family. Once the bond had been formed, we were quite inseparable. We did not have an official clique per say but we were a bunch of buds hanging out as one, Larry, Pete, Stanley, and the Hall clan. After our 1971 graduation he and I were supposed to enlist in the army under the buddy system. One buddy chickened out and Speedy spent two years in Hawaii without me. Some of my wildest and craziest times were with Speedy and this supporting cast of genuine friends. The last time I saw him was at our 40th high school reunion. We kept in touch through FB though. Speedy gained his wings May 14, 2020, sixty-seven years young when a drunk driving a pickup swerved across the centerline and hit him head on while he was social distancing himself as he called it, riding his Harley a few miles from home.

We relocated from Abbeville to Myrtle Beach in 2005 where I had started a new job in Conway a hop and a skip away. Rebooting, I had to not only learn the terrain of my new position but also make new friends. Of my newfound wonderful friendships, one had been that of a coworker, Frances Woodberry. It is odd how friendships develop but we did become amazing friends. She was so easy to talk to and we talked about almost anything. She was a true friend. I was still working parttime at Metglas when I shared the news with her of how losing Sammy had impacted me and had launched me into my first relationship with God.

A bit of her life was shared in a book I penned. She had shared this mysterious story about her childhood. She and her sisters had lived in terror at an old planation home that her parents rented and farmed. Something haunted that house on Port Harrelson Road and it visited her and her sisters' rooms regularly at night when they were children. This is no spoiler alert as I will not be divulging the storyline here. To read this compellingly haunting tale depicted in the 60s in Bucksport, S.C. you must purchase, borrow, or steal a copy of The Hardwood Walker of Port Harrelson Road. At the young age of sixty-six, my dear friend died October 9, 2020 at home while on her computer of what I have heard might have been a heart attack or stroke. The good ones leave us way too early but knowing her, she is sporting those wings proudly.

This brings me to Ed McMenamin, obviously not a hometown southern acquaintance with a name like that. Excluding the Civil War, Abbeville was not exactly Yankee territory during my life there. Ed was born in Philadelphia. I met him on a golf course in Murrells Inlet January 2016. After retiring at the end of 2015, I was not the rocking chair type. I enjoyed playing golf, but my usual golfing buddies were still working and usually not available for play until the weekend. I decided to fill this void by playing weekly at Tupelo Bay in Murrells Inlet, an 18-hole executive golf course, a mixture of par 3s and short par 4s. During my second round of solo play a twosome ahead invited me to join them. Ed and his pal Martin played there weekly. From that day we became a threesome playing one to three times each week, the birth of the Tupelo Boys. I became the southern center between two Yankee slices of bread.

I was introduced to extremely slow play; not easy for me being a fast pace player. Even quirkier, they took two cracker breaks during the round, always on the same two holes. Not wishing to defy the customary style of play I began bringing crackers to the course. Over the next three years an assortment of characters joined us rounding out a foursome most days. Ed had more health issues than anyone I have ever known. He shared his printed list with me just prior to scheduled surgery for leg circulation issues. I think the list included almost any serious health issue you could possibly have and an equally impressive laundry list of removed organs. Never had I ever seen such a list and the person sharing them still alive.

The arrival of Covid 19 stymied our regularly scheduled rounds. I bowed out first because of my age and preexisting conditions, diabetes, figuring I would sit on the sidelines for a while. Ed died May 31, 2020 at age seventy-seven due to breathing complications, one of the many health scenarios documented on his list. Covid was not involved. July of 2020, one of our remaining Tupelo Boys regulars, Marvin, built a house in Fayetteville, West Virginia and moved away. Martin, one of the original founding fathers, had long ago moved back north. I last played with Ed Feb 24th. A creature of habit, I bet Ed did not easily warm up to wearing wings but, if I know him, he probably introduced God to the cracker break concept. Covid 19 is indeed a terrible and scary disease but everyone does not necessarily die from it. Every death should not be categorized with having links to Covid. People do still die from other causes. Or at least they used to.

Befriending these three is represented over a unique span. My life with Speedy represents the pre-Covid and my Pre-God era. With Frances, we shared a pre-Covid timeframe, but she was there for me when I began developing my relationship with the Lord. Ed showed me how mere strangers on the links could develop an unexpected kinship. We did not talk about God or share any spiritual stories, but he was truly one of God's walking miracles. With all the health intrusions he had incurred God kept him around for years well beyond what could have been a short stay on this earth. God's plan is His plan and we never know exactly why He does what He does in our lives. Ed filled a void when I was in need of having one filled.

I read this saying somewhere and it just seems appropriate.

Let Go of all that weighs you down.
Heal those broken wings with love
Because one day you will fly again.

2020 A Year Unlike Any Other

I never began my journal journey thinking that 2020 would come into play for anything more than documenting my progress in the spiritual realm. This pandemic has been a game changer for many reasons. Who would ever have envisioned we would still be in a shutdown scenario ten months later and still battling Covid 19? Who would ever have thought that there would be those in our county, in our government that would utilize this crisis to forward their socialist agenda? Fear and deception are powerful tools, but God is still the Almighty. Like the virus still wreaking havoc on humanity, my journey continues as well. Government pushes us relentlessly. God pulls me effortlessly.

The big box stores like Costco, Sam's, Best Buy, Home Depot and Lowes remain in operation, essentially dubbed. Walmart, Target, liquor stores and strip joints are essential. God's house of worship is apparently still nonessential, nonexistent in some states. Protests and rioting are still acceptable. Thanksgiving and Christmas gatherings are dangerous. They tell us to stay at home, social distance, wear masks and wash our hands and then they have the audacity to then tell us not to gather as family in our homes. Are we safer inside or out and why is it safe to be shoulder to shoulder in the aisles of big box stores but unsafe to be in the aisles of churches? It is all about controlling the flock, owning us, ruling us, making us dependent on government and less dependent on the love of God. God terrifies them. Faith scares them. Us believing in the Lord upsets their plans to rule us with them as the golden idols for us to worship them for controlling every aspect of our worthless lives. We are supposed to remove God from politics and schools but ironically it is God who can save us from the ruthless politicians.

My journey, this journal was never envisioned as being an outlet for anything more than my personal awakening to a relationship with God. 2020 invaded that premise. Still, I held firm to my faith. I heeded the pull and continued my quest to be a better person, a child of God, a believer in miracles and the Almighty Creator, on a journey even a year like no other. The harshness of reality can dish out cruel consequences that can pose obstacles to any spiritual journey. Covid, along with the government and scientific community have been devilish challengers in a world turned upside down. Through Biblical times far worse scenarios have evolved to test man's faith in God. God has come out on top every single time. I see this as a mere challenge with the same outcome. God wins in a blowout and so do we.

My personal journey is not over and realistically it probably will never be. I don't think it is supposed to because there is so much yet to learn and experience. Some have spent a lifetime with such a relationship. Mine began well into the backside of life. I continue praying and reading my devotionals, staying true to that promise to myself and to Him. It is my proverbial 'cross to bear' and no one else's. My way is not always pretty and I still stumble off the righteous path from time to time, but I have never lost focus on the ultimate goal and in my heart I never will. Sure, I will be tested. Sometimes I will pass with flying colors. Other times I might fall on my face. Trials and tribulations are thusly so. You learn from them. You hope to avoid making the same mistake. You move on. If it were easy the world would have been healed long ago. God's work would be complete. We know and He knows that His work will never be complete. There are too many pigheaded nonbelievers out there, too much hatred, too many of Satan's aimless sheep to promise us a world without worry. And the old devil will never forgo his quest to be the only one worthy of being worshiped. Evil searches for the slightest opening, a crack to slime its way into our lives and for any sign that we are disenchanted with God. Ironically, like the political arena, carrots are constantly dangled in front of us, promising free stuff to win us over. Nothing is free in life, not possessions, money, or a soul. Think otherwise and you have fallen into the addiction meant to own you and ruin your life.

Again, I am no expert in these matters. I am but one sheep doing my best to follow the Godly flock. I believe in Him now. I trust Him. I love Him. I am not without flaws though. As I have said before, I will stumble. I will fall. I will be tempted, and every opportunity will be offered to snatch me off the wagon, sometimes during the spiritual ride. I am convinced that I will recognize it when it happens and reconcile it to the best of my ability. Perfection is not a human quality. Imperfection rules our world, the one He created for us. We are His children and as children go, we do not always do as our Father wishes we would do. We will make mistakes and sometimes we do require disciplinary action. He knows exactly how to handle these matters when His children misbehave and exactly what is required to delivery us from evil. Sometimes children deserve discipline. Our job is to listen and do what He asks us to do.

Do I talk to Him? Not exactly. I do pray and in a sense that is talk. Does he talk back? No, I have never heard Him speak. I have never seen Him. Just because I have not heard or seen Him does not mean He is not real. This is a poor analogy and I apologize up front for even saying it. I have never seen Bigfoot. Does that mean that the illusive Sasquatch does not exist? There are those that swear this creature exists. It is not for me to judge those that believe in its existence. Some people feel the same way about UFOs. Again, I am not comparing God's existence to Sasquatch or space invaders, just saying that we should never question someone's beliefs. Christians should not be persecuted for believing in God. Just that simple in my humble little pea brain. It is not easy for me to think and share such thoughts. Not ashamed by any stretch but I am not sure I have had skin in the game long enough to express on any philosophical level.

Cuz, Sammy Cannon got the ball rolling in quite an unimaginable way, through his death. After losing that battle with leukemia he gained his wings and then tossed out a life preserver to me. I stand firm by these thoughts. Yours to believe or not. The sequence of dominoes fell and led me to where I am. Far from over but as is Sammy, I too am in a better place on earth as he is in heaven. Scary what the world is becoming while I attempt to navigate my way through a world I never really knew existed. I got the God part years ago. I just did not have Him in my part.

My journey started after Sammy's earthly one ended. Never could I have envisioned the countless defining moments and transformations that an old guy like me would experience. From dreams to church firsts, all inspiring and wonderfully different. Timing is everything and I am sincerely thankful that my relationship with the Lord had begun before 2020 arrived. With Covid and the world gone politically crazy and angry I cannot fathom where my mind and heart might be right now if I had did not have God in my life. I still struggle when I pray with all this going on around us. It is so easy to just ask God to wave his mighty hand and fix it. In our prayers we are supposed to ask him, right? He knows best and I suppose praying that He does what He sees right for us is the better prayer. With so much deception and hatred in our country and the world it is tough to imagine there is a simple fix for any of it. The world has always been at odds. I do not see it changing in my short lifetime. Then, what do I really know? God has engineered an endless supply of miracles and has punished the world when need be. One cannot help but wonder if we have reached one of those punishable offenses.

I will have no control over what happens in the biggest of pictures so I shall end this on a happy note. Thank you, Cuz, for pushing me into God's pull. I will always be indebted to you, for giving me life from your death. Scary. Sounds a bit familiar. Realistically, I know Sammy did not sacrifice his life for me in the biblical sense. I still credit him with opening my heart and my eyes for greater things. My heart goes out to his bride, his Judy, for I know she misses him every single moment of every single day. And to his children, her children and the grandchildren who miss having Poppy in their lives. As for me, my journey into the pull continues and I pray that I too will earn my wings and one day be reunited with the Lord our Savior and see those angelic faces that now reside in His Kingdom. Until then, I will do my best to talk the talk and walk the walk as God wishes for all of us to do. God is Good.

Treasure Hunts and Treasure Troves

Just when you think it is over, my last entry I mean, it isn't. I had decided ending this with my previous thoughts. The new year 2021 had a curve ball to toss my way though. Extraordinary powers can lead you down unexpected paths. The pull is that powerful for sure. January 19, 2021, as I sat in the sunroom sipping my first cup of coffee, an urgent pull entered my mind and then my heart. It beckoned me to the built-in bookshelves in the living room. No. I was not being pulled blindly. I knew instantly where I was going and what I intended to retrieve. I had seen them weeks ago when cleaning out the enclosed storage area beneath the bookshelves. The dual cabinet doors had become a catch all for this and that but also concealed hidden treasures.

Inside I had found two bibles. One had my mama's name inscribed on it and the other had my parent's names inscribed on the front. Both were obviously old and tattered. Mama's had been given to her Jan 23, 1940 given the handwritten note inside. I can only assume that the other one inscribed with Mr. and Mrs. Thomas J. Winn must have been given to my parents when they married. Mama had received hers from her parents, John and Ruby Bowie that day in 1940 at the age of 9 years and three months according to the dedication. Oddly, neither Papa or Granny could read or write so it remains a mystery who wrote the note for them.

There was a third bible, this one located on one of the shelves. It had belonged to Granny Bowie. Here I had three bibles, one belonging to Mama, one to Mama and Daddy and the third to Granny Bowie, and I had never read or opened any of them to this very day. If I had, I have no memory of it. Given my history I had never been inclined to open or read from a bible. I am not even sure that I ever received a bible as a child. I have no recollection of it if it happened. Now I sit here starring at three,

A Hank Williams Sr. song written in 1946, a song titled *Dust on the Bible* goes like this,

I went into a home one day to see
some friends of mine
Of all their books and magazines, not a
Bible could I find
I asked them for the Bible when they
brought it, what a shame
For the dust was covered o'er, not a
fingerprint was plain.

Dust on the bible, dust on the Holy word
the words of all the prophets and the
sayings of our Lord
Of all the other books you'll find, there's
none salvation holds
Get the dust off the Bible and redeem
your poor soul.
Oh, you can read your magazines of love
and tragic things
But not one word of Bible verse, and the
sayings of our Lord
Of all the other books you'll find, there's
none salvation holds
Get the dust off the Bible and redeem
your poor soul.

Oh, if you have a friend you'd like to help
along life's way
Just tell him that the Good Book shows a
mortal how to pray
The best advice to give him that will make
his burdens light
Is the dust on the family bible trades the
wrong way for the right.

Dust on the Bible, Dust on the Holy Word
the word of all the prophets, and the
sayings of the Lord
Of all the other books you'll find, there's
none salvation holds

217

Get the dust off the Bible and redeem
your poor soul.

Could be it is my time to dust off a Bible. I have three to choose
from so it seems. I opened the one given my parents, a larger Bible
than the version presented to Mama. There were no handwritten
notes inside. Did Daddy or Mama ever read from it? That I will
never know. Did Mama use hers? Given the fact she had been
presented it when she was nine and still under Papa and Granny's
reign, I would almost guarantee she had. Maybe she even read it to
them. I can only hope she did. Funny, I do not remember the Bible
being read to me when I was a child. I am not saying it wasn't but I
can not recall a single time if ever it was. Might be too much dust on
this old brain.

This brings me to the third Bible, the one I can only assume
belonged to Granny Bowie. The page presented to, by, and date were
blank. The tip off to ownership spoke proudly and clearly by the
treasure trove of items concealed inside. Granny had kept various
items that meant something to her. There were book markers,
clippings, obituary items, photos, and other mementoes. As I have
previously stated, she could not read nor write, so many of these
must have been read to her by Mama or others and she insisted on
keeping them. I have included a few while keeping all of them.

From the Treasure Trove
(Granny with sisters and parents)

Great Grands Papa and Granny Holmes (seated)
Granny Bowie (second from the right standing)
I recognize Aunt Lucy kneeling far right,
Aunt Nelly standing far left with Aunt Sallie Lou beside her
Not sure about the rest.

Granny Holmes and Papa Holmes Standing
Aunt Jennette and Uncle Junior (Granny Bowie's Brother)
With three of their children

BOB WINN

LIKE AN OLD OAK TREE,
STOOD STRONG IN THE WIND.
HE COULD NOT BE BROKEN,
AND HE REFUSED TO BEND.

LIKE THE ROOTS OF A TREE
HIS MEMORY WILL RUN DEEP.
HE WEATHERED ALL STORMS
AND HIS FAITH HE DID KEEP.

I designed and wrote this tribute to Bob, my Judy's son, after his death in 1990, losing his battle with cancer.

IN LOVING MEMORY

John R. Bowie
ABBEVILLE — John R. Bowie, 90, of 904 S. Main St., died Feb. 13, 1990, at his home.

He was a retired painter and retired employee of Abbeville Mills. He was a member of the Pentecostal Holiness church.

Surviving are his wife, Ruby Holmes Bowie of the home; a daughter, Mary B. Winn of Abbeville; and a sister, Ida Blanchett of Summerville.

Services: 3 p.m. Thursday at the Pentecostal Holiness Church with burial in Forest Lawn Memory Gardens.

The family is at the residence.

Memorials may be made to the Pentecostal Holiness Church, 113 Barnett St., Abbeville 29620. — Harris Funeral Home, Abbeville.

Papa's book marker after his death

FINALLY HOME. . . . .
For years he had waited
In discomfort and pain,
Living life day by day
With but one thing to gain.

A wonderful Christian
A true man of God,
Patiently awaiting
His final reward.

While on earth he touched many lives,
His heart withered, but sweet.
He gave to everyone his fullest –
We called him "Papa Pete."

Things changed one Saturday morning –
March 18, a sorrowful and grieving time.
It hurt so much 'cause we loved him,
To us it was such a crime.

The thought of burying my Papa
Made me cry and sob with grief;
And the only thought that consoles me
Is knowing that Papa's at peace.
(Tribute to "Papa Pete" by Anna Norris)

Tribute to Pete Bowie by Anna Norris after his death
Pete was Granny's nephew, highly respected and loved
by family and friends.

REJOICE IN THE LORD

Rejoice in the Lord always.
I will say it again:
Rejoice! Let your
gentleness be evident
to all. The Lord is near.
Do not be anxious about
anything, but in everything,
by prayer and petition,
with thanksgiving,
present your requests to
God. And the peace of God,
which transcends all
understanding, will guard
your hearts and your minds
in Christ Jesus.

— Philippians 4:4-7 NIV

This card was among her many little treasures.

Thank God For You

Thank God for you,
- good friend of mine,
Seldom is friendship such as thine:
How very much I wish to be
As helpful as you've been to me—
THANK GOD FOR YOU.

Of many prayer guests, one thou art
On whom I ask God to impart
Rich blessings from
- His storehouse rare,
And grant to you His gracious care—
THANK GOD FOR YOU.

When I recall, from time to time,
How you inspired this heart of mine:
I find myself inclined to pray,
"God bless my friend this very day—
THANK GOD FOR YOU.

So often, at the throne of grace,
There comes a picture of your face:
And, then instinctively, I pray
That God may guide you all the way—
THANK GOD FOR YOU.

Some day I hope with you to stand
Before the throne at God's right hand,
And say to you—at journey's end,
"Praise God,
- you've been to me a friend--"
THANK GOD FOR YOU

A poem by
Dr. Joseph Clark

She kept this one too-*Thank God for You*
A poem by Joseph Clark

I have often said that Granny Bowie was the closet person I have ever know to being a saint. She believed and worshiped the Lord with all her heart. Her Bible stuffed with these little treasure troves is testament to this fact. There were many other little goodies squirreled away in her Bible, too many to include and only she knew why she kept some of them. I handpicked a few to share as I knocked the dust off her Bible.

This brings me back to the other two Bibles. The one gifted to Mama and Daddy held no treasures, nothing hidden within the pages nor any scribblings. It is a keepsake just the same, one obviously forgotten and ignored until now. I have choices. Which one will I claim as mine for the journey ahead? Obviously, they already belong to me so claiming them is a poor choice of words. Selecting one is quite easy though. A no brainer. My draft choice is Mama's Bible. She received it in 1940 at age nine. In a sense I am a mere child at age sixty-seven. Seems appropriate I begin my journey through the pages of hers. And now you know the rest of the story, or at least the story up until now.

Theirs and Hers

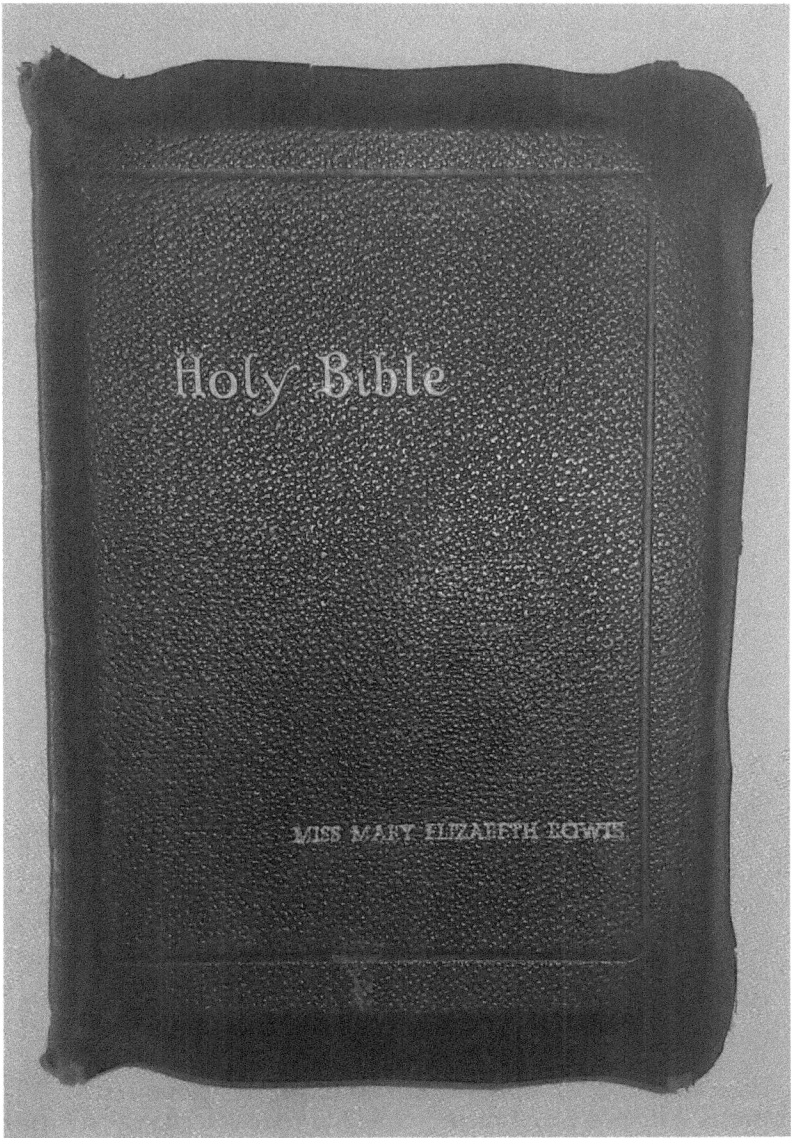

A Sacred Token

To Mary Elizabeth.
Bowie. Age 9 yrs 3 mths.

From Mother & Daddy.
As a Birthday Gift.
Let this precious Book be a
Light to your pathway and a lamp
to your feet. And give your heart to
God while you are young and always
Walk the shining Gospel Way.
Date Jan. 23, 1940.

Thomas Allen Winn January 19, 2021 Re-Birth Age 67 and 9 months.

This passage is from John Wesley, English cleric, theologian and evangelist, a leader of a revival movement within the Church of England known as Methodism.

Jesus, who now art passing by,
Our Prophet, Priest, and King thou art:
Hear a poor unbeliever's cry,
And heal the blindness of my heart:
Urging my passionate request,
Thy pardoning mercy I implore, Whoe'er
Rebuke I will not rest,
Till thou my spirit's sight restore.

One of his quotes: ***Though I am always in haste, I am never in a hurry.***

I liken this to being in the pull as Paster Buddy said, there is no time frame for getting there and no right or wrong way. In due time all things will pass so is His plan for me.

An Unlikely Devotional Pull

Sometimes life is full of surprises, often from the unlikeliest places. I do intend to allow Judy Cannon to proof this book. First, I figured I would reread it now that I had a printed copy in hand. Sometimes you see things in print that may have gone unnoticed on the laptop screen. I began reading it unintentionally in my morning devotional slot. Almost like an out of body experience. It was as if I was reading another author's work because this writing was unlike anything I had ever written. If not for the references about Cuz or experiences I recognized, it could have been authored by someone else. Not bragging, but it might be my best work so far. I found myself learning the lessons I had already lived and learning while being lifted to even loftier heights in new lessons being learned. I had hoped my experience would inspire others and here I am being inspired by it as well.

Living this new life and writing about it was something I had not envisioned doing. Publishing it and sharing it with the world is beyond anything I ever imagined. Held in God's pull like a tractor beam from the Starship Enterprise was totally unexpected. Wow, reading what I wrote is quite miraculous given who I was and the road I traveled for nearly sixty-five years. Again, I am not tooting my horn. On the contrary, I am blowing the trumpets for everyone to hear. Look at me! If I can get this, if I can do this, if I can embrace it, love it, and live it then anyone can. Hopefully, for you it need not come at the expense of losing someone you loved. It should not be caused by something tragic. Then again, we do not always have the luxury of choosing our destiny and the path better traveled, do we? I am proof of this fact. At your own time, at your own pace, no right or wrong way to get there so said Pastor Buddy, there is nothing better than starting that relationship with God.

Many begin the process early in life. Family and maybe friends help build the foundation. It doesn't mean that there aren't plenty of late bloomers out there like me. Sometimes the foundation might require an extreme home makeover. Sometimes you could be a mere fixer upper. Wherever you might be in life, it is never too late for

232

redemption. God is powerful and ready to lend a helping hand. I was pushed but I needed to be pushed. Without that little shove I might not have arrived to where I am now. Losing Cuz left me without a happy place and seeking answers. Stumbling and falling is not a pretty sight. Wandering aimlessly is not a good feeling either. Think about the blind people Jesus cured. In my own way I was blind, but He opened my eyes. When He did, I saw things clearly, more vividly than I ever had.

Scary awakening! I just glanced at my smart watch and realized my step count was at 666. I launched to my feet to take a few quick steps. While 687 steps are not a healthy count and far from my daily goal, it looked extremely better, more comforting than those three devilish numerals. I am not superstitious but tempting fate is not recommended. Never ignore obvious signs I say. Satan, possibly realizing that I was caught in God's pull, decided he needed to distract me and yank me in his direction. Sorry old man, your sign of the beast is no match for the pull and the One tugging the reigns. I made plenty of bad decisions all for the sake of fun and outrageous reward, but those times are long gone. Even at my worst I would have never bought into demonic behavior. If I were going to worship anyone it would have never been you. There is a fine line between hypocrisy and Christianity. I attended church off and on but refused to live the life of the hypocrite when I was not in church. I sat on the sidelines when attending, understanding I was not on solid ground in the Lord's house, but I was not going to pretend to be righteous when my heart was not in the right place.

You cannot be a part time Christian. I get this. I got it all along. I never pretended to be something that I wasn't. No harm, no foul so I thought all these years. The entries in my journal certainly held back no punches where this was concerned. Reading them again certainly reinforces these facts, where I was then and where I am now. Love lifted me. Amazingly so, I have come a long way, an incredibly long way. It sounds like I am the only one that has ever experienced this transformation. In a way this is correct. I never really paid any attention to anyone else who professed to have found God. I did not previously exist in that world. It did not interest me, nor did it hold my interest. My life was my life. Yours did not impact mine, or at least I did not allow it within my comfort zone.

Interestingly though, beating the dead horse, my writings do paint a unique picture, the analogy of the blind man and the one touched by God, the wakening. Unique might be a bit overdramatically stated. I am the furthest thing from being unique and my experience is only unique because it altered my world. He shook it to its proverbial foundation. It is not easy living in the same house your entire life and then having to build a new home from the ground up. Here I am doing just that. Instead of my house it is God's house. Mine was beyond being a mere fixer upper. It was demo day big time. Daily devotions keep me on track. Lessons learned keep it real. Life is Good. God is Good. Cuz believed in this mantra. Keeping Cuz's legacy alive I do as well.

I began reading Jesus Calling, borrowing my Judy's copy of the book. On February 28th, the devotional hit home. Here is an excerpt.

> *Stop judging and evaluating yourself, for this is not your role. Above all, stop comparing yourself with other people. This produces feelings of pride or inferiority, sometimes a mixture of both. I lead each of My children along a path that is uniquely tailor-made for him or her. Comparing is not only wrong; it is also meaningless. Don't look for affirmation in the wrong places: your own evaluation or those of other people. The only source is affirmation is My unconditional Love.*

I think back on how people close to me have often compared me to others, mostly wishing I were not me and more like those others. My defense has always been I am who I am and do not aspire to be like anyone else. Part of my push back persona and pigheadedness. I wish I had known about the above words years ago but then again that predated my relationship with the Lord. It might have helped me, and helped others understand where God stood on the subject and me being tailor-made by Him just as every other individual is what they are by design, not choice. I am an old dog capable of learning a few new tricks as discovered in my relationship with God

234

I now have. Like me or dislike me, I am unique as are you. We were never supposed to be alike nor ever expected to think and act the same ways. What is important is living the life He intended us to live. My route in getting here was a long and winding one of misdirection and plenty of detours and obstacles to overcome. I finally arrived though at my pace and my way, uniquely speaking. The road ahead should be interesting and fulfilling.

Pushed into An Epilogue

The magnetic pull cannot be swayed or influenced with the change of a year. No denying it, the year 2020 offered its fair share of unpredictable challenges. The push and the pull met these obstacles head on with plenty of opportunities for me to bend if I allowed myself to be impacted by the deceit and devastation in abundant supply, but I never broke from the iconic tractor beam tugging me toward the center of the universe, God's universe. My 2021 routine remains regimented, perfected as Pastor Buddy once advised me, prayer before bedtime and allotted time for devotion in the mornings. I cannot deny that the occasional hiccup does occur in the mornings devotionally speaking. I pray the Lord forgives me for these brief breaks in my daily promise to myself and to Him. Perfection is not part of the human DNA unfortunately.

Ending 2020, I completed my second round of reading Men of the Bible Pastor Buddy so graciously gave me. Starting out the new year I have been jumping from one to another, a series of books I have downloaded from Amazon onto my Kindle. I am trying to map a new route, still mostly searching right now. After I stumbled upon my mom's bible, I still intend to begin my first ever reading of the scripture from her bible. It is in my 'around to' pile right now. Well, I am sixty-seven and a half now and have been on the right path for a while, thank you again Sammy Cannon, for pushing me into the pull. I regret that my new life began when yours ended. Death for you, re-birth for me.

I focused much of my time in the earlier version of my journal on you and those dreams you appeared in, visits to me to apparently put things in perspective. I reached a stopping point at the end of 2020 when I was led to publish the journal. I miss those dream visits and lessons you taught me. I have not had a dream of you in an exceptionally long time now. I guess either God or you decided I no longer needed that crutch or divine guidance. My bet is on God. After all, he does pull the heavenly strings. I am sure you have settled in simply fine there in heaven. I wonder who is keeping that list for you, the one I maintained so that you would not forget items like golf gloves, golf shoes, balls and sometimes something as significant as your golf bag when we played a round on the links. A part of you is with me every time I play. No, it is not just memories; I wear your golf Garmin to guide me around the course. Your Judy saw fit to bestow it on me after your death. She gave me plenty of your golf balls and a marker hat clip. I treasure these knowing they once belonged to My Brother. I have your 15-club as well, but I have not perfected its use, not nearly as accurate as you were when you strategically pulled it from the bag. Cuz, your Judy enclosed a beautifully written card when she so graciously gave me these items.

Tommy,

I wanted you to have something special of Sammy's. He was like a child at Christmas when I gave him his golf course GPS. I know in heart he would want you to have it. I am also throwing in some golf balls and his little 'thingy' he wore on his visor.

You and Sammy had a special bond. I knew no other man he cared more about. I am so thankful for that. You'll never know how much he appreciated and enjoyed your time with him in the hospital.

He was a special a man and he held my heart in the palm of his hand. God blessed us all when he gave us Sammy.

I Love you,

Judy

So just where am I in this incredible journey, walking in the light of the Lord? The pull remains persistent. Your push is no longer required, Cuz. Your job is done, thank you very much. Do not dessert me yet though. An angel is always welcome as my wingman. Suite 101 is still yours, the spare bedroom known forever as your home away from home. Sometimes I think I can still hear your yells of 'Cuzy, Tom-mey or cold beer!' Miss those references and distinctive tone of your voice. Yep, you made a forever impact on my life, but I would not wish to be the one responsible for giving you a heavenly big head. God might not appreciate my interference or influence. I drift off point so it seems. Thinking of you tends to send me on that memory lane path. Not a bad thing but it can distract me somewhat.

Let me try this one more time. Where do I find my life all these years later, a life that began shortly after your death? Currently my journal is ready to be proofed. Your Judy saw a post from me on Face Book on the Beach Author Network where I announced the rollout of *Pushed into the Pull*. My bad, I had failed to give her a heads up that I had written it and intended to publish it. She was taken aback and all for good reasons. She even offered to proof it for me. I think this is a perfect ending. She added that she knew you would love it, saying she could almost envision you looking down from heaven and saying, 'Pour me one more beer in the funnel, Cuz.' She still remembers that time you were working on my irrigation well pump in Pawelys Island when I was your gopher and would tilt back your head, tell you to open your mouth like a baby bird in a nest while I poured beer down your gullet. I did not want to disrupt your work on our pump. Here I go again, digressing. Judy 2s fault this time, not mine.

During Judy's proofing process, she sent me a link to a song that she said reminded her of me. The song is Love Broke Through by TobyMac. Here are the lyrics.

I was feelin' that, feelin' that breeze
Singin' like a song thru the tall oak trees
It was just another summer night
Had to be the last thing on my mind
Yeah, I was all but lost in the moment
I was young and runnin' wide open
It was just another summer night
Had to be the last thing on my mind
When love broke thru
You found me in the darkness
Wanderin' thru the desert
I was a hopeless fool
Now I'm hopelessly devoted
My chains are broken
And it all began with You
When love broke thru
And it all began with You
When love broke thru

I did all that I could to undo me
But You loved me enough to pursue me
Yeah, You drew me out of the shadows
Made me believe that I mattered, to You (You)
You were there, You heard my prayer in that broke down dusty room
It was the first time I said, "I'm Yours"
The first time I called You Lord
When love broke thru
You found me in the darkness
Wanderin' thru the desert
I was a hopeless fool
Now I'm hopelessly devoted
My chains are broken
And it all began with You
When love broke thru
And it all began with You
When love broke thru
Yeah, it was late in the summer when the northeast breeze
Sang like a song thru the oak trees
Pennsylvania
She kind of caught my soul
Which had me a little more open than closed
Walls I built
Opinions I learned
Covered in the ashes of bridges I burned
Blind to the arrow that headed to my heart
But You hit the mark
When love broke thru
You found me in the darkness
Wanderin' thru the desert

I was a hopeless fool
Now I'm hopelessly devoted
My chains are broken
And it all began with You
When love broke thru
When love broke thru
You found me in the darkness
Wanderin' thru the desert
I was a hopeless fool
Now I'm hopelessly devoted
My chains are broken
And it all began with You
When love broke thru
And it all began with You
When love broke thru
I did all that I could to undo me
But You loved me enough to pursue me.

Songwriters: Toby Mckeehan, Chris Stevens, Bryan Fowler, Bart Marshall Millard

Sometimes an ending has not exactly ended. Through a re-editing and reissuing exercise for this previously released book I stumbled into a gifted surprise. I had began reading Judy's copy of *Jesus Calling* in 2011, a new path heeding to the pull. Today April 30th I discovered a unique and heartwarming note written 2018 by my Judy on the daily devotion. No explanation is required as I have photographed and pasted it below. God is forever good.

April 30

WHEN SOME BASIC NEED IS LACKING—

time, energy, money—consider yourself blessed. Your very lack is an opportunity to latch onto Me in unashamed dependence. When you begin a day with inadequate resources, you must concentrate your efforts on the present moment. This is where you are meant to live—in the present. It is the place where I always await you. Awareness of your inadequacy is a rich blessing, training you to rely wholeheartedly on Me.

The truth is that self-sufficiency is a myth perpetuated by pride and temporary success. Health and wealth can disappear instantly, as can life itself. Rejoice in your insufficiency, knowing that *My Power is made perfect in weakness.*

JAMES 1:2–3; 2 CORINTHIANS 12:9 NASB

Tommy Christ
accepted
today!
Praise God!!
4/18

125

About T. Allen Winn T. Allen

Winn began writing in 2003 while being cooped up in hotels during business travel. Completing a 650 page so called novel he became hooked. The homegrown Abbeville, S.C. boy embraced the experience completing one novel and then leaping into the next one, fun and therapy at the time. That changed in 2011 when a chance encounter brought stranger and new neighbor Bob O'Brien to his Pawley's Island doorsteps. Bob did not realize the neighborhood home had been sold and apologized when Tom greeted him instead of the man he had expected to see. Book in hand, Bob had just published his first novel, The Toppled Pawn and explained the previous neighbor had shown interest in writing. Tom remarked he dabbled in writing to which Bob asked, do you have a manuscript? Tom replied 'ten'. Bob had just started Prose Press, a publishing company and suggested publishing one. You cannot make this stuff up.

T. Allen Winn's first novel, Road Rage joined the ranks of the published a few months later, and he owes a special thanks to Bob O'Brien for making this possible. His first seven books were published by Prose Press. In 2016, T. Allen Winn established Buttermilk Books, his publishing company and has now published twenty-two books under the brand. He and his wife reside in Myrtle Beach, South Carolina.

Ole T does not write a specific genre. He writes what strikes his fancy. If you don't see something that fits your reading wheelhouse, just tell him what you like, and he might just write it for you.

Books are available on Amazon or online where books are sold. Select books are available at Southern Succotash on Washington Street in Abbeville, S.C. and in Tabor City, N.C. at Grapefull Sisters Vineyard. Or *Message* T. Allen Winn on Facebook to arrange delivery of signed copies, or to schedule him to speak at an event or book club.

Fiction from T. Allen Winn

The Detective Trudy Wagner series

Road Rage
North of the Border
Tithes and Offerings

Bigfoot Trilogy

Book 1: Foot, Tree Knockers and Rock Throwers
Book 2: Another Foot, What Really Happened to D.B. Cooper

More Fiction from T. Allen Winn

The Perfect Spook House
Dark Thirty
Lou Who
Raw Ride, a Wild West Zombie Apocalyptic Shoot'um Up
The Man Who Met the Mouse
Mister Twix Mystery, a Cat Scene Investigation
Come Here, Getouttahere, Tyler's Tail Wagging Tale
The Tenth Elemental
Last Stand on the Grand Strand
The Lord's Last Acres
Covert 19, 2020 A Devil of a Year

Non-Fiction from T. Allen Winn

Being Bentley, A Dog Like No Other
It's All About the 'A', Faith, Family, Football and Forever to Thee
with coauthor, Benji Greeson
It's All About the Angels in the Backfield, Dawn of a Dynasty
with coauthor, Benji Greeson
December's Darkest Day, While I Breathe, I Hope
The Hardwood Walker of
Port Harrelson Road (based on true events in Bucksport, S.C.)
Cuz, My Brother, Life is Good, God is Good
Pushed into The Pull, Thank You Cuz

Memoirs

Vol 1: The Caregiver's Son, Outside the Window Looking In
Cornbread and Buttermilk, Good Ole Fashion Home
Cooked Nostalgic Nonsense
Vol 2: Don't Sit Naked in a Grits Tree, More Nostalgic Nonsense
The Endless Mulligan, Short Shots from the Golf Whomper

Biographies

Clay Page, Somewhere In Between
Screw It, Let's Ride, The Legend Bub Lollis

Short Stories

For Your Amusement featured in Beach Author Network's
book titled 'Shorts'

Ciled Me a Bar featured in friend and author, Danny Kuhn's
Headline Book's
Mountain Mysts, Honorable Mention in Fiction at the 2015 London
Book Festival
and the book is endorsed by *Joyce Dewitt* of the sitcom *Three's
Company*

Short story about Granny Bowie in friend and author Robert Sharpe's book, *The Heart and Soul of Caring*, about caregivers and their challenges